HOW TO
KEEP YOUR
C.O.O.L.
WITH YOUR
KIDS

HOW TO KEEP YOUR C.O.O.L. WITH YOUR KIDS

Learning to Be Better Parents by Controlling Our Own Lives

Lou Makarowski, Ph.D.

A PERIGEE BOOK

The diagnostic criteria for Attention-Deficit/Hyperactivity Disorder, Conduct Disorder, and Oppositional Defiant Disorder appearing in the Appendix are taken from the American Psychiatric Association's *Diagnostic and Statistical Manual of Mental Disorders, Fourth Edition,* Washington DC, 1994, and are used by permission of the American Psychiatric Association.

A Perigee Book
Published by The Berkley Publishing Group
200 Madison Avenue
New York, NY 10016

Copyright © 1996 by Lou Makarowski
Book design by Irving Perkins Associates
Cover design by Sheryl Kagan

First edition: April 1996

Published simultaneously in Canada.

The Putnam Berkley World Wide Web site address is http://www.berkley.com

Library of Congress Cataloging-in-Publication Data

Makarowski, Lou.
    How to keep your C.O.O.L. with your kids : learning to be better
parents by controlling our own lives / Lou Makarowski.
        p.   cm.
    "A Perigee Book."
    ISBN 0-399-51991-2
    1. Parenting.   2. Parents—Psychology.   3. Anger.   I. Title.
HQ755.83.M35   1996
649'. 1—dc20   95-23049

Printed in the United States of America

10 9 8 7 6 5 4 3 2 1

This book is dedicated to the memory of my mother, Roseanna Healy Walsh Makarowski, who in life and death has been an unwavering source of love and inspiration. My father, Louis William Makarowski, who taught me the value of work and the importance of character.

To Marilyn, my friend since 10th grade, wife, lover, and helpmate. My children: Kimberley, whose love and laughter have lighted my life; Kristen, whose untimely death taught me the value of life; and Michael, my son, who is the bravest, most kind-hearted person I have ever known.

Lastly to my grandparents, uncles, and aunts, who always made me feel special, and to all those who have provided support and encouragement throughout my life.

A sincere thank you to all, and God bless.

Acknowledgments

I would like to recognize and express my appreciation to Marilyn Herrmann Makarowski for the enormous contribution she made to this book. Without her help as sounding board, primary typist, and editorial assistant, this book simply wouldn't exist.

All my teachers, but particularly the late Daniel Brower, Ph.D., of Montclair State College, Vinton Rowley, Ph.D., of the University of Iowa, Richard Bealka, M.D., of the J. O. Cromwell Children's Psychiatric Hospital, Independence, Iowa, and psychoanalyst Saturino S. Ortega, M.D., of Cedar Rapids, Iowa.

Friends who reviewed and assisted with early drafts of the manuscript include Robert Wilson, M.D., Henry Doenlen, M.D., Richard Sullivan, Ph.D., Jerry Foote, Frances Yeo, and Larry Day, Ph.D. Thank you!

A special note of thanks to the nationally and internationally prominent physicians, psychologists, and others who sent letters of support documenting the need for a book such as this one. Those who offered invaluable advice which helped shape the final draft include Jerry Deffenbacher, Ph.D., Harvey Parker, Ph.D., Ronald Friedman, Ph.D., Dennis Harper, Ph.D., and Frank Cranley.

Those who also offered professional reviews and support include Russell Barkley, Ph.D., Redford Williams, M.D., and Keith Conners, Ph.D.

Thanks to senior editor Irene Prokop for her vision, way with words, and professionalism. She and her staff at Perigee have been a pleasure to work with.

Special thanks to my agent, Peter Rubie, who guided me through all phases of the development and production of this, my first, book.

Contents

Foreword

This is a book about how to deal with losing your temper when your children have pushed you to the limit. Parents who suspect their children are hyperactive, overactive, or just plain aggravating should read this book. It will teach you to control yourself so you can discover a far richer and more enjoyable relationship with your children, who will also learn from your example. Parents of high-maintenance children, those with ADHD (attention deficit hyperactivity disorder), for example, will find this information invaluable.

Think of *How to Keep Your C.O.O.L. with Your Kids* as a toolbox for parents. You won't find a hammer, saw, or Allen wrench hidden between the pages, but you will find the tools you need to tame your temper. Then, when little Allen, Sawyer, or Hammer does his best "Dennis the Menace" imitation, you will be prepared. You will have the tools you need to change angry, hostile confrontations into positive experiences.

The whole idea of this book is to help you develop effective ways of dealing with children who always seem to make you mad. *Mad*— now there's a word that is loaded with surplus meaning. Webster's dictionary says that mad can mean insanity, mental illness, frantic with fear, foolish and rash, infatuation, wildly amusing, having rabies as in a mad dog, or an angry mood. Not very flattering company for our angry moods, I daresay. Who among us wants to be known as a madwoman or madman? Even fewer would choose to live in a madhouse. I can't think of a single person who would say that a madhouse makes a good environment in which to raise children.

The secret to keeping your C.O.O.L. is learning how to deal with yourself. Wouldn't you really rather respond to annoying children in a manner that is calm, composed, and marked by control of emotions? Of course you would. I have yet to meet the mom or dad who wants to make their children miserable. The most important thing harried, frustrated parents can do, both for themselves and for their children, is to learn what causes them to be so angry and how to change it. As you read on, you will learn the few simple skills you will need to increase the happy times and decrease the unhappy ones.

This book will be most helpful if you follow these steps:

- Complete the Anger Quotient Survey at the end of this chapter. It will help you to determine the scope of your problems with anger.
- Take the C.O.O.L. Parent Quiz in Chapter One. It is designed to help you realize the wide range of options available to you now that you have determined that you must change. Some of the questions might surprise you, but your answers will introduce you to many of the C.O.O.L. tools that are explained throughout the book.
- Give the entire book a quick read. Familiarize yourself with the overall approach. The big picture will help you to understand how change occurs. The process of exchanging hostile for healthy involves learning to consider the context, objectively observing yourself, organizing your options for productive problem solving, and looking to the future while learning from the past and living in the present. The C.O.O.L. skills themselves will teach you how to make it happen. What the tools are and how and why they work will be explained thoroughly.
- Begin practicing the basics of anger management. Arousal control is the key. Practice cool breathing and deep muscle relaxation until you can relax on cue when you are alone. Practice using arousal control in situations that don't involve your children. Recognize how tense you become when treated rudely by a coworker or a clerk in a store, for example. By practicing anger management away from your children, you will be better prepared to respond effectively when your children push your hot buttons.
- Begin to monitor your thoughts that trigger anger. I call your thoughts self-talk. What you say to yourself will have a great deal to do with your motivation and success. When you develop the ability to scan your body and mind for the early signs of anger, analyzing situations more objectively will become natural to you. This will reduce anger's ability to distort your

thoughts. As you learn to reframe your self-talk and calm your body, you will be better prepared to use these tools to construct a more loving relationship with your children and a more positive image of yourself. Soon you will not only recognize anger in the early stages, you will also be able to prevent the hostile reactions that hurt your children.

When implementing any skill or child development tool, the rule of thumb is to start with the easy ones first, and when you have experienced success, move on to the more difficult ones. Then, slowly but surely, you will begin to see how progress can be made.

ANGER QUOTIENT

Read the following statements and indicate your level of agreement with each one:

Strongly Agree 1	*Agree* 2	*Disagree* 3	*Strongly Disagree* 4

1. _____ There are very few people who care how I feel.

2. _____ When angry, I hit more often than I intend to.

3. _____ My kids make me furious.

4. _____ I have very little confidence in my ability to control anger.

5. _____ When angry, I use foul language too often.

6. _____ When angry, I hit harder than I intend to.

7. _____ I have a hard time apologizing.

8. _____ I often lash out at others.

9. _____ People take advantage of me too often.

10. _____ I have instant anger more often than I should for no good reason.

11. _____ When my kids defy me, I get furious.

12. _____ I often feel ashamed of the way I behave when angry.

13. _____ My friends say I have an anger problem.

14. _____ I often lose control when angry.

15. _____ I try to stop my anger, but can't.

16. _____ I make decisions or punishments when angry that I change after I cool off.

17. _____ I frequently get in fights over discipline.

18. _____ I can't stop arguing even if I want to.

19. _____ I fear I might hurt those I get angry at.

20. _____ Talking to my kids is a waste of time.

_____ TOTAL

Total your score to determine your anger quotient at this time. This is a personal measure designed to help you evaluate the scope of your problem with anger. It will also be a useful way to check your progress as you master the art of effective problem solving when worried sick about your children. It's not a pretty sight but all of us have been there at one time or another, angry adults acting like children.

Moms and dads usually come to my office with these questions: "Why does my child behave this way? What must I do to bring about change? Is my child hyperactive? Does she need medication?" But regardless of the questions, the answers all parents want are ways to cope with the challenges of modern parenting.

The trend these days is to medicate or warehouse unruly children in psychiatric hospitals or halfway houses because teachers, caregivers, or parents can't cope, or don't want to cope. Such treatment of children and adolescents, in many cases, is not only wrong but ethically dubious and unnecessary. And the explanation of why a child behaves the way he does depends on who is doing the explaining.

Medical explanations of behavior and personality are currently the most popular. That is why there is so much emphasis on treating behavior with medicine these days. Medical doctors are trained to believe that some underlying physical disease—a latent cause, if you will—is responsible for the behavior disorders they are asked to treat. So, naturally, they prescribe methods to treat this. Psychoactive drugs are by far the most common treatment by medically inclined psychiatrists, pediatricians and family physicians. For true mental illness, there is no more effective treatment.

No amount of kind words or environmental manipulations will cause a schizophrenic to stop hallucinating. That person needs medicine to change his or her brain chemistry and stop the hallucinations and delusions of grandeur. The same is true for severe mania, attention deficit hyperactivity disorder (ADHD), psychotic depression, and several other disorders.

But typical emotional disturbance in children is most efficiently treated by a combination of psychological support, insight, advice, and skill training, not pills. Most mood and anxiety disorders are effectively treated with psychotherapy and environmental manipulation. And while medicine may play a part, skills stick with you; medicinal cures typically stop when the medicine is withdrawn.

All serious scientists agree that hereditary predispositions to aberrant behavior exist. Most of our personality is inherited. They normally agree that a few of these behaviors are clearly the result of disorders of the brain's chemistry, but the disagreement comes with how many syndromes and how much deviance from typical or normal is required before we have a right to label someone with a "lifetime" diagnosis of a mental disease or behavioral disorder.

Children given ADHD or conduct disorder labels tend to be quarrelsome, hyperactive, impulsive, inattentive, and disrespectful. For our purposes, we can define some of them as children who consistently have difficulty doing what they are told to do. In a sense you could say that they don't exist in the same kind of world as the rest of us.

Often, however, the problem is not the child, but the situations he or she is being expected to cope with that are in need of change. The conduct disorders that drive you mad occur in a context of massive social upheaval in America. Divorce alone produces depression or defiant disorders in most adolescent boys for a year or more.

If you believe your child is developing a conduct disorder, *do something about it now*. Conduct disorders might result from a combination of genetic predisposition, poor supervision, and emotional, arbitrary, and inconsistent discipline. Most of these factors are a direct result of our changing moral and cultural climate, a climate that puts children and child rearing last on the list of importance. These problems are largely the result of decisions, not diseases.

Likewise, if your child has been diagnosed as having ADD (attention deficit disorder) or ADHD, then you will want to know how improved parenting skills can help you cope with frustrating behavior, and this book will teach you that. Since ADD and ADHD are two of the more popular labels currently given to behavior disorders of children, we should take a closer look at what they mean. According to Dr. Russell Barkley, a neuropsychologist at the University of Massachusetts Medical Center who has studied ADHD and related disorders for more than twenty years, true ADHD is a permanent disability: a neurodevelopment disorder. Those who have ADHD lack what it takes to keep still, persist at boring tasks, or delay gratification. They fail to organize themselves, control their emotions, or empathize with others at a level normally seen in children their age. At times they are delightful, but not for long. They are very moody.

ADHD is not an attention disorder at all, but rather "an impairment in inhibiting behavior." Dr. Barkley believes the name ADHD is actually a misnomer. These kids annoy others and are destructive to themselves. Often accident-prone, if they develop a negative, defiant attitude as well, they have a terrible future outlook. Their brains lack the ability to allow them to stop and use their memory. Exactly what is wrong with their brains is not well understood at this time. Some people acquire the disorder as a result of injury or disease, but that number is very small. ADHD itself is not a disease per se; it is a trait people are born with. As with intelligence, for instance, some have more and others less.

An excess of this trait produces very inconsistent behavior and temperament. This is what usually drives adults mad. On some days, in some situations, the child will do exactly what is expected; yet, in a similar situation, his or her behavior is so inappropriate you want to scream.

The deficit is not a moral failing, reaction to diet, or the result of poor home training. These kids are at the extremes of a trail we all possess. Western society's increasing emphasis on doing more with less time seems to make the problem worse as well.

ADHD is by far the psychiatric disorder most likely to be inherited.

In some clinics specializing in the treatment of ADHD, 25 to 40 percent of the parents of ADHD children have this disorder themselves.

True ADHD kids are almost always born with a lack of the ability to do automatically what most of us take for granted: to profit from mistakes. They crave novelty. When something attracts them, they rarely stop and think about the consequences or what happened in similar situations before. They just do it. What it is doesn't matter a whole lot to them.

As infants they are often cranky. As toddlers they have high activity levels and language and coordination problems. By the time they are five and six years old, their poor judgment, inability to organize themselves, terrible handwriting, and conflicts with authority take center stage. During elementary school they wear out their welcome with their peers and struggle with math. Many get hostile. After puberty the truly hyperactive child has few "normal" friends and the boys are so immature they have trouble finding girlfriends. The girls, on the other hand, have such poor judgment that many become promiscuous and, too often, pregnant. When it comes to driving, the record of these kids is atrocious.

The good news is that severe ADHD only affects between 3 and 5 percent of the population. That is the number who meet the current criteria for clinical diagnosis of attention deficit hyperactivity disorder. Boys outnumber girls from 3 to 1 up to 9 to 1, depending on the setting in which the data is collected.

The bad news is that up to 57 percent of the population will have some of these symptoms to a noticeable degree. That is a cultural phenomenon and practical issue of enormous significance. The extent to which the larger group is considered deviant or different is largely a value decision. Teachers identify the symptoms much more often than psychologists. In one study reported on by Dr. Wiley Rasbury, teacher ratings suggestive of ADD/ADHD approached 60 percent of the referrals to his clinic, but no more than 3 percent of these children actually received the diagnosis.

Attention deficit disorder is very different from ADHD. Like ADHD, it is a disorder of brain function, but a different part of the brain is involved, and ADD shows itself in different ways. ADD kids are often dreamy, introverts, shy wallflower types, very unlike the driven, aggressive extroverts with ADHD. These kids generally do much better in all areas. They require far less of a support system than hyperactive children.

An ADD child has an information processing deficit, in contrast to an ADHD child, who has an inhibition deficit. ADD is indeed a true attention disorder.

But even normal children driven to distraction by unsafe or unfit educational environments will increasingly be misdiagnosed by professionals and parents concerned about their inability to concentrate. Why?

Significant portions of our education system have been recognized as failing. Virtually all reputable authorities agree that schools need to change. Urban schools are often the worst. Being certain our children are being taught in an organized, professional environment is a difficult task for parents today. No wonder we get angry! The environmental factors influencing behavior are more than we're equipped to handle, and school is the one place where we expect our children to be safe.

What about the number of children in the classroom? Is thirty to thirty-five children an appropriate number? In my opinion, the answer is no! Twenty to twenty-five children is an appropriate class size for so-called normal children. You say your grandparents had fifty children in a class and they did okay. That may be true, but the children in your grandparents' classroom had only *read* of divorce and broken homes. They had an extended family network that kept watch over them. They came home from school to a mother who was available to them. If they forgot their lunch, Mom could come up to the school and bring it to them. Grandma's kids brought to school a different set of attitudes toward authority. They were encouraged to be more respectful to authority. Today's kids may rely on Bart Simpson for a role model. Teachers have become the Rodney Dangerfields of modern society: "They don't get no respect."

It would be very naive to assume that the changes in modern society have not encouraged children to question, challenge, or even defy established rules. Certainly the teacher's task of educating adventurous and spirited children is more difficult than was the case a generation or two ago. Mark Twain's perspective on education offers all of us some food for thought. He believed that we should "never let school interfere too much with a child's education." Today, respect for authority is taught from a different textbook than the one you or your parents used when you were in school.

Consider another aspect: the classroom tasks to which the child is asked to pay attention. When children are assigned work sheet after work sheet throughout the day, the ethical question becomes Is this an appropriate learning environment for any child? Certainly, the more curious children will become more active in this environment. They get bored—wouldn't you? Should the environment be changed or should the children be sedated? We also have a question of teacher competence. Is your child's teacher providing an appropriate educational environment for your youngster? Can your child's teacher spell, speak, and write with correct English and grammar? Shouldn't we expect that, at least?

Fear, uncertainty, anxiety, depression, and worry all play important roles in increasing your child's emotional stimulation as well. When we experience unpleasant emotions, our bodies and minds become very active. Increased stimulation leads to increased activity and distractibility. Stimulation may come from within a child's mind or heart. The child who brings a heavy heart to school is going to be more easily distracted than one who brings a light heart and an open mind.

Modifying the child's environment to make it much more user-friendly will help tremendously. That's what this book is all about.

If you have a high maintenance child, he or she will need help to develop a healthy social network. Often these kids turn just about everybody off. The loneliness they feel makes them particularly vulnerable to the influence of negative peer cultures. As they grow into adolescence, the only teenagers that will accept a disruptive, impulsive underachiever are those with similar problems. Or worse, those who prey on these lonely kids, offering promises of friendship in return for "favors" that could break their heart or put them behind bars. School counselors and teachers must have input. Teachers must be involved, informed, and kept up-to-date if they are to do their part effectively.

Brothers, sisters, and peers must be considered, not so much as part of the problem, as for ways in which they might be part of the solution. I often find that family therapy helps all family members keep their C.O.O.L. There may also be other factors, such as relatives' attitudes toward your child, specific learning disabilities, or times of increased family stress that contribute to your child's activity level and inability to concentrate.

So when the question of using medication to modify behavior comes up, understand that there are a lot of issues involved. Medication can be an important aspect of a multimodal approach, but it shouldn't be the whole treatment. Children treated with medication do get better conduct grades and report cards. Oddly, their scores on standardized tests of academic achievement change very little. Take the advice of experts, but take it with a grain of salt. Quality care is a shared responsibility.

I wrote this book because I was unable to find a book to give to the families I work with as a practicing psychologist, a book that would teach them how to kick the anger/hostility habit. Parenting books do a good job of telling you how to handle your child's behavior. They do a lousy job of telling you how to handle your own emotions. Anger sneaks up on us. Too often, we find ourselves so angry that we forget to use the skills we have learned from the parenting book; before we know it, we are furious. Our fury is destructive, disappointing, and oftentimes depressing. Sometimes people are angry and don't even realize it; these people are especially susceptible to what I call flash anger.

How to Keep Your C.O.O.L. with Your Kids will teach you the process of recognizing, relaxing, reframing, and then responding productively to potentially unhealthy situations, regardless of their cause. This is a proactive approach to parenting. The anger control tools in this book are useful to anyone—parent or not. You can't control your emotions, but you can control your reactions to them. Learn how to "get a grip!" in the pages that follow.

The Anger Quotient Survey is a quick way to help you recognize your overall potential to behave in destructive ways when you feel angry. It will help reduce flash anger. Too many families suffer from the disastrous effects of improper methods of expressing themselves. Consistently they have told me that this review has helped them to focus their attention on what they want to change about their response to angry feelings, regardless of the source. Arbitrary, inconsistent anger expressed to children in hostile ways is one of the main reasons children develop serious mental, social, and legal problems.

The examples in this book were drawn from actual case histories. At the time I wrote it, I had completed more than fifty thousand hours of psychotherapy, counseling, and psychological evaluation with children, adolescents, and adults. In all of the examples used, the names, situations, and other identifying information have been changed to ensure the complete confidentiality of my clients.

PART ONE

THE PARENT

CHAPTER 1

Becoming a
C.O.O.L. Parent

"Why can't I take Jason somewhere without always being embarrassed by having to yell at him?" "Why am I such a grouch so much of the time?" "Why does my child act this way?"

Sound familiar? Then I have written this book for you! Let's begin where a lot of books and classes about effective parenting of a difficult child never seem to spend much time—with you. The C.O.O.L. parent system is designed to help put more love and laughter in your life. It teaches you the skills you will need to problem solve when your anger is provoked by your children or others. As your problem-solving skills increase, you will be less vulnerable to self-defeating power struggles and flash anger. C.O.O.L. parents have the skills to make the hard choices about correct behavior. Throughout the book, you will be learning skills that will provide you with practical, useful ways to deescalate situations that trigger your anger. *C.O.O.L. stands for Control Our Own Lives.* C.O.O.L. parents are committed to trying to make healthy choices in tense situations. To do this they:

C—Consider the context and consequences of their reactions to provocative situations that trigger their anger;

O—Observe their breathing, body tension, and communication objectively;

O—Organize options for successful problem solving when provoked;

L—Look to the future, learn from the past, and live in the present.

They see themselves as they want to be and learn to lighten up with confidence. Learning to lighten up will actually make your children more, rather than less, compliant. Please don't misunderstand. A C.O.O.L. parent is *not* a weak parent. But when love is not enough, the C.O.O.L. parent has the skills needed to keep the relationship alive, so that he or she can love another day.

As we study anger and how it affects our bodies, our relationships, and our work, we learn that anger and cynicism both make us more vulnerable to heart attack, cancer, and virtually all manner of health problems. Loneliness is the invisible price of a "successful" life that is lived on an epinephrine rush of anger. Studies of highly successful senior citizens have consistently revealed their regret at not having invested more of themselves in their relationships with loved ones and friends. Others driven by rigid, polarizing behavior patterns, which result from an inability to empathize, relax, and build positive relationships, experience lower levels of personal achievement in all areas. The human costs of anger in terms of personal unhappiness are simply staggering. Dr. Ed Diener and his colleagues at the University of Illinois have studied traits of happy people. Their work has reinforced my belief that fun and happiness are powerful medicine for our emotional and physical health. Preliminary results from my own research indicate that maintaining the fun factor in life will reduce stress, depression, and anxiety. Approaching the anger problem from a fresh, new perspective of what makes and keeps us happy leads researchers to concur with Benjamin Franklin when he surmised that "happiness is produced not so much by great pieces of good fortune that seldom happen as by little advantages that occur every day." Over twenty years as a psychologist have led me to agree that the fun factor is an important part of keeping C.O.O.L. The fun factor makes an important contribution to reducing anger, anxiety, guilt, and other negative emotions, and supportive, intimate relationships are among life's greatest joys.

Cooling your temper helps you to build those relationships. The best insurance policy you can provide for your child's future is to promote a family environment that is characterized by mutual love, respect, and happiness. After reviewing the results of thousands of studies that span the globe, Dr. Diener found four traits that seem the most potent predictors of personal happiness: self-esteem, a sense of personal control, optimism, and extroversion.

The C.O.O.L. parenting system promotes these traits in both yourself and your children. Happiness is an important antidote to anger because happy people like themselves and are liked by others. Children want to please happy parents. Happy moms and dads set realistic, achievable goals for their children that allow everyone to be both affectionate and loving. These parents can't help but be pleased with themselves and their children most of the time. A happy environment promotes initiative by creating an attitude of "can do" instead of "do I have to?"

A strong sense of personal control will allow you to feel happy because you will be less threatened by difficult or challenging situations and better able to cope with any stresses they may provide.

Happiness is reinforced by your optimism and your child's initiative. How many of your conflicts with your children are rooted in their failure to "see what needs to be done and do it without being told"?

Extroversion is a kind of initiative. Extroverted individuals reach out more to others, are more comfortable being team players, can ask for help when they need it, and can ask others to do their bidding when that makes more sense. They tend to be high-spirited and less anxious. They marry sooner, get better jobs, and make more friends. Confidence in your child's ability to succeed will do wonders to help you look past tense moments and worries about his or her future. Visions of your successful children won't hurt your self-esteem as a good mom and dad either.

Another important tool for the C.O.O.L. parent to understand is the role of temperament in shaping your relationships with your child. The great debate in human development has raged for centuries. At issue is the extent to which our personalities are the result of inherited temperaments or traits, and the extent to which they are the result of how we are raised as children. I mention this because it is obvious to anyone who has spent much time around children that some of the children's traits are just like Mom or Dad, Grandma or Aunt Nell. However, many researchers believe that personality traits such as introversion or extroversion are determined before birth.

B. F. Skinner, the father of operant conditioning and behavior modification, freely acknowledged the role of genetics in the development of personality traits, while the famous Swiss physician-psychologist Carl Jung believed that people are predisposed to develop *relative* preferences for four different types of mental processes: sensing, intuition, thinking and judging. The C.O.O.L. parent has no axe to grind with either side of the nature/nurture debate.

Whether you or your child tend to extroversion or introversion, don't get hung up on the labels. One thing that behavioral science knows for sure is that whenever scientists group people's traits and categorize them, the differences among the people *within* any one category is always greater than the average difference *between* two different groups. So, statistically, when you compare introverts with extroverts, for example, you will discover broad areas of similarity between individual members of the two groups.

The reason I find these concepts useful in the area of anger management is that frequently there are mismatches within families. Extrovert parents and an introverted child, for example, could lay the groundwork for a lot of misunderstanding and miscommunication. The same is true if we have an extrovert husband and introvert wife.

The introvert draws energy from within. Introverted adults prefer to be alone at the end of the day. Solitude energizes them and they prefer to get lost in a TV show, cleaning, or reading a book—any of which would bore an extrovert to tears.

Extroverts draw energy from people, for example by socializing with others, talking, laughing, and cutting up at the end of the day. Being mindful of how the members of your family prefer to recharge and relax may help you decide when to push your point and when to back off and give them some space. Proper use of interpersonal space can help you avoid escalating an irritating incident into a major family war.

Being a C.O.O.L. parent begins with an analysis of ourselves. Reflecting on the choices you habitually make when you're angry will increase your awareness of what you are doing that is working well and point out what needs work. Reflecting on how your choices are seen by your children, spouse, or close friends can also motivate you to change. Forming a mental picture of what success *could be*, in an ideal sense, helps you to achieve it.

First, get a handle on your actions and reactions by taking the following quiz.

C.O.O.L. Parent Quiz

Circle the number that best describes your level of agreement with the following 25 ways to complete this statement: "When I get angry with my child, I act after _____ "

Strongly Agree 1	*Agree* 2	*Disagree* 3	*Strongly Disagree* 4

When I get angry with my child, I act after ___

(1)   1   2   3   4   I analyze the situation to consider the context of my child's behavior.

(2)   1   2   3   4   I check my anger arousal level or TEMPERature.

(3)   1   2   3   4   I am sure of my ability to treat my child with love and respect while I investigate the context of the incident.

(4)   1   2   3   4   I take time out, away from my child, until I am certain that I can treat my child with love and respect.

(5)   1   2   3   4   I identify the thought or behavior that triggered my anger.

(6)   1   2   3   4   I check to see if my anger was triggered by something or someone other than my child.

(7)   1   2   3   4   I communicate calming words to myself.

(8)   1   2   3   4   I breathe deeply from my diaphragm to provide maximum oxygen to my brain.

(9)   1   2   3   4   I scan my body to identify excess muscle tension.

(10)   1   2   3   4   I release all unnecessary muscle tension.

(11) 1 2 3 4   I remind myself to communicate with constructive body language to my child.

(12) 1 2 3 4   I remind myself to move slowly toward my child.

(13) 1 2 3 4   I remind myself to speak softly to my child.

(14) 1 2 3 4   I see myself (in my mind's eye) productively interacting with my child.

(15) 1 2 3 4   I identify the belief, standard, or value I hold dear that my child has violated.

(16) 1 2 3 4   I recall a time that I personally violated that belief, standard, or value myself.

(17) 1 2 3 4   I recall a time in my childhood (my child's current age) that I made a mistake similar to the one I am angry about.

(18) 1 2 3 4   I communicate with constructive words to my child.

(19) 1 2 3 4   I see myself (in my mind's eye) productively interacting with my spouse or significant other. (If single, score 2.)

(20) 1 2 3 4   I communicate with constructive words to my spouse or significant other. (If single, score 2.)

(21) 1 2 3 4   I choose a consequence strictly for its potential to increase the probability that my child will make a better decision next time.

(22) 1 2 3 4   I am sober and not under the influence of alcohol or mind-altering drugs.

(23) 1 2 3 4   I have satisfied my body's needs for rest, pain relief, food, and drink.

(24) 1   2   3   4   I am satisfied that the consequence will not make me feel powerful at the expense of my child's self-esteem.

(25) 1   2   3   4   I evaluate my ability to treat my child with love and respect while I administer discipline.

Please take the time to answer the C.O.O.L. Parent Quiz. This will help you find out how successful you are in managing your anger. You may also find it helpful to ask a friend whose judgment you trust implicitly to complete the quiz with you in mind. A friend can provide useful information from a different vantage point. Some of my clients have even found it useful to review this quiz with their children. Others have gone so far as to complete the items as they believe their child might have. Angry exchanges in families are reduced when the children are exposed to C.O.O.L. rules. This assessment will also give you a bench mark, a measure of your overall progress. It will serve to jog your memory and help you review your C.O.O.L. skills from time to time. Two or three months from now, after you have read this book, you may find yourself backsliding a bit. Simply retaking the C.O.O.L. quiz will remind you of healthy options for problem solving that you may have forgotten. This process will also trigger emotions, ideas, and strategies that will help bring you back to C.O.O.L. living. At a minimum, I recommend that you reassess yourself halfway through the book and again at the end. Periodic reassessment is also an indirect way of encouraging a C.O.O.L. lifestyle.

Parents who know that they get angry too often tell me that simply completing the C.O.O.L. Parent Quiz can be a powerful emotional experience. As they reflect on the history of their interactions with their children, emotional memories are often triggered. You, too, may experience a variety of emotions, but don't be disappointed if this doesn't happen. For some, this experience is energizing, but others find it irritating. Inner turmoil, embarrassment, or shame are not unusual reactions of first-time quiz takers. Equally common are feelings of pride, a sense of accomplishment, or a newly discovered confidence that can only come from knowing that you have learned how to tame the beast within. Your emotional reaction to the questions can help motivate you to move from denial or simplistic thinking about the need for change to actually making a commitment and acting on it.

You have many opportunities and choices when your anger is aroused. The C.O.O.L. Parent Quiz will help you to identify several of the more important ones that will be explained and illustrated in the chapters that follow. The items in this quiz were designed to offer a virtual menu of alternatives. As you answer the questions remember that a C.O.O.L. parent is one who uses one or more of the steps, depending on what he or she discovers works best for the parent and his or her children in their very own situation. No one, certainly not me, could expect a parent to go through all twenty-five steps before acting.

This survey is the first of your anger-management tools and will help you gauge your progress as you master the other tools of the C.O.O.L. process. Use it.

CHAPTER 2

Diagnosing Behavior and High-Maintenance Children

Before we get into the specifics of keeping your C.O.O.L., let's take a closer look at childhood behavior and misbehavior. Sometimes children are unruly—that's just part of being a kid. But sometimes our children require high maintenance. That's when parents as well as teachers are quick to suspect hyperactivity and attention disorders. A diagnosis of hyperactivity, or more correctly, Attention Deficit Hyperactivity Disorder (ADHD), should only be made by a team of professionals. This team should be composed of you (the parent), a psychologist, a medical doctor, school counselor and your child's teachers. Sometimes other specialists will be added to the team. A psychologist is trained to evaluate and recognize the many different causes of hyperactive, challenging, or otherwise disturbing behavior. There are specific steps in this evaluation process. The child with ADHD has trouble staying still and staying on one task for a large amount of time, far more so than other children of comparable age in the same learning situation. ADHD results from a physical abnormality in the brain's functioning. The consistent inability of the child to remember to use what he or she knows lies at the core of what appears to be self-absorbed, driven emotionality. A thorough developmental history will reveal that the problems with focus, organization, and inhibiting impulses were apparent from infancy, unless the brain was damaged by illness or accident afterward.

Some children with concentration problems, especially girls, are *not* hyperactive. This type of concentration trouble is called Attention Deficit Disorder or ADD. There are many problems, some physical, some personal, others resulting from school or family conflicts, that can cause children to manifest a lot of "nervous energy" and annoying behavior as well. The techniques and tools in *How to Keep Your C.O.O.L. with Your Kids* will help you to be a more effective and loving parent no matter what causes your child's disturbing behavior. The specific criteria used to diagnose ADHD and ADD are presented in the Appendix, so if you suspect you have a child who fits into the high-maintenance group, be sure to read the guidelines presented there. But let's also look at behavior from a child's point of view.

Annoying kids get smiled at less than others. And, from the day they are born, some children are more annoying than most. These children often get scolded for normal, exploratory behavior that is age appropriate. They learn at a very early age to be sensitive to criticism because they are criticized so frequently. If little Brittany is in the kitchen playing with pots and pans, a parent is likely to smile at Brittany and be proud that she's showing an interest in useful activities. But if it's little Chad in the kitchen destroying the cupboard, you're more likely to scream, plug your ears and close your eyes, or worry that he'll pull the pot of boiling water off the stove on top of himself while wrecking the kitchen.

The panic you feel as a parent almost from the beginning of this child's life creates a tremendous barrier. The positive bond can even be absent. It is not that you don't love your child, but there is an absence of a relaxed environment, so strain is always in the air. As an infant, toddler, and preschooler, Chad has learned that he is offensive to practically everybody. He cannot understand it, and he certainly can't verbalize it. He just has an unpleasant feeling most other children rarely experience. You feel uncomfortable, too, afraid of your temper, afraid of your emotions because your reactions to your child scare you, particularly if this is a first child.

Often parents don't feel maternal or paternal instincts. Instead, they just don't want to be around their child very much. You love your child, but you can't stand to be around him or her for too long. You even feel guilty about this, but that doesn't help you or your child. Instead, let's think about behavior patterns.

In the beginning, before you had a child, you had yourself, your family, and you may have even had your temper. I know it didn't seem as bad as it is now, but a large percentage of provocative children do come from parents who are themselves hyperactive, depressed, nervous, or compulsive. Think back to your own school years. Were you a class clown? Did you have difficulty learning? Were you a talker, daydreamer, procrastinator, or perfectionist? If you weren't yourself, ask these same questions about your child's other parent. I'm really asking this: Is "Dennis the Menace" part of your personal history or the history of your spouse? Could either of you have filled in for his scriptwriters? If Dennis doesn't describe either one of you, think about these other possibilities:

1. Do you have a short fuse?
2. Are you sometimes accused of being mad at the world?
3. Do friends see you as stressed out or always on the go?
4. Are you the impatient one in your group?
5. Are you from a dysfunctional family yourself?
6. Are you very moody?
7. Do you finish your friends' sentences because they talk too slow?

A yes answer to any of these statements could indicate that one or both of you will benefit from patience training.

We all want our children to be happy and successful. When they're not, when their success or viability is threatened, we worry. As parents, we try to protect our children. But how do we react when we ourselves are a danger to our children because we become too angry or too irritable too often? When we are destroying the very self-esteem we want to nourish, we parents feel terrible!

Lindsay, for example, felt terrible about her temper. Every time she lost it, she felt guilty and attacked herself. She accused herself of being a rotten person. In time, her assaults on herself became unbearable. Her need to feel adequate as a mom caused her to shift some of the pain to others. Before long Lindsay began to blame those closest to her. Blaming her friends and family was one way Lindsay could reduce the painful feelings she experienced. Did she blame her loved ones on purpose? Of course not. Lindsay's blame was not the result of a plan. It was the result of her emotional pain. Her cruel, hostile words came automatically, subconsciously, if you will. She did not even realize she was blaming others until after her rage was spent. We all blame others sometimes, but Lindsay found herself blaming others nearly all the time. She blamed her spouse, other children in the neighborhood, or the school system. She externalized responsibility and blamed others because it hurt too much to think she was the main reason her child did not experience the success she had envisioned for him.

Too often, we blame ourselves, letting our emotions and our ignorance get in the way. Mothers wonder, "Is it my fault? Could I have taken better care of myself during pregnancy? Should I have demanded better prenatal care?" Fathers think, "Did he inherit this temper from me?" These days we read a lot about chemical imbalances causing problems with behavior. Some experts claim these chemical imbalances can be inherited from parents. In the case of ADHD and specific learning disabilities, we know this is true. Even cigarette smoking and alcohol are linked to ADHD, but most of us don't realize this until it's too late. However, it remains true that no normal parent wants to hurt his or her child!

Danielle, for example, knows the pain of rejection and condemnation. Her mother, an alcoholic, had vitriolic fits of temper. Her scathing remarks left Danielle scarred for life. Rings of self-doubt rule Danielle's life. She believes she has no right to speak her mind or to be taken seriously when she does. Predictably, Danielle's frustrations mount. Volcanic explosions of anger, rage, frustration, and fear periodically erupt. Typically, her children's misbehavior triggers her rage. A message of hate and discontent covers those she loves with the grime and soot of her fury. Confused by mixed messages of love and hate, her children and loved ones experience fear, self-doubt, and confusion.

Allie, Danielle's youngest, vows silently to be a better child. Allie, who is eight years old, is beginning to feel guilty for upsetting Mommy. When the aftershock subsides, Danielle feels the pain of shame, remorse, and self-doubt. "How could I be so cruel?" Danielle has become the mom she never wanted to be. Danielle doesn't like herself very much. Sometimes Danielle's outbursts serve to scare her children into doing the kind of things she wants them to do, but only for a little while. Then, Danielle feels extreme guilt, depression, and shame. "How could I do this to these kids? I sound just like my mother."

One thing that made a huge difference for Danielle was her decision to find a healthier role model. Her mom was an excellent negative role model. Danielle learned just about everything she did not want to be from her mother. Now she needed a positive model. Someone whose cool demeanor would illuminate the path of change. A neighbor's anger style caught her eye. Regardless of what happened, Linda always made it a point to remain calm. No matter how creative her children became at pulling her chain, she rarely let them know that it bothered her.

A picture is worth a thousand words when it comes to control of anger. Who comes to mind when you think of a C.O.O.L. person? Whom do you look up to as a role model because they are in Control Of their Own Lives? Name someone you admire because he or she appears to be all that you hope to become where anger is concerned.

You might want to list the qualities of this person you admire most. Then name one quality you possess that reminds you of your role model.

Name one change you can make today to be more like your role model.

Danielle began to grow out of her history. Soon after moving next door to Linda, she started to change the hostility habit. Other skills helped, but her decision to select a positive role model was a giant first step in the right direction for Danielle. The energy that once demolished her daughter Allie's self-esteem was transformed into constructive activities that laid a solid foundation for her positive self-image.

Parents need to realize that anger is an emotion, a feeling. Nothing more, nothing less. You can't control what you feel, but you can control your actions. Anger is neither a sin, nor a justification. It's simply a feeling. Anger is inevitable. If you are raising a difficult youngster, you are going to be angry. If you are raising a high-maintenance child, you are going to be more angry, more often. Anger is a natural, healthy emotion which needs to be handled in a healthy way. Healthy anger never changes into physical attacks or demeaning verbal assaults. Brief anger is the best anger. If you can let go of anger and move on, it is usually healthy. Each new day should start with a clean anger inventory. Vendettas and long-term grudges are the results of unhealthy anger. Healthy anger leads to problem-solving strategies. When you can speak to the person you are angry at and make a good-faith effort to settle the conflict or agree to drop it, your anger is healthy. Hostility and aggression, however, reflect unhealthy anger. As I use the term, hostility involves malice, spite, and ill will. A disposition to injure is very much a part of the definition of malicious behavior.

Aggression is an action or set of actions that an individual sometimes takes when he or she experiences anger. Hostile thoughts frequently precede or justify aggression. Aggression is an attack, either verbal or physical. Hostility can be an attitudinal component of aggression. It is rooted in cynicism, suspicion, and resentment. Aggression frequently involves a failure to act at all. Ignoring a person you know on the street or failure to shake an extended hand is most certainly a hostile action. Such behavior is called passive hostility or passive aggression. Of course not all aggression involves anger. Crimes or wars, for example, may occur for purely economic reasons. But parents holler at and hit their kids almost always out of an automatic flash anger, and that type of behavior is what this book will help you change.

Aggression and hostility don't lead to healthy patterns of problem solving. The use of controlled force is sometimes necessary in the family, but hostility or malicious aggression have no place in a healthy family system.

Consider an example. Hank and Larry live on the same block and sell insurance for rival companies. Their 13-year-old daughters have played softball at the same park for years. This year, Tracy and Camille play for the Lady Tigers. Both girls are trying out for the same position, second base. Sue, the girls' softball coach, works for the same insurance firm as Larry. This is causing a problem. Larry has been lobbying hard. He's hoping Sue will let his daughter, Camille, play second base. When Sue puts Camille ahead of Hank's daughter Tracy, Hank is furious. Meanwhile, Keith, Sue's husband, meets Hank at the local deli, smiles and extends his hand in greeting. Hank stiffens and walks right by. Keith is puzzled. Later Hank feels like a fool as he tells his wife what happened. "I was just so angry. I know he and Sue talked about the girls' assignments. I can't stand to be a hypocrite. I am mad as a hornet about this. I just couldn't shake his hand."

Passive aggression can be one of the most frustrating experiences a parent has to deal with. Taking out the trash provides many families ample opportunity to fight passively. Consider the case of Barry and his mom, Lindsay. "Barry, will you please take the trash out? I'm going to take a bath and the dog has been sniffing around it. I'd hate for him to get into that barbecue we had for dinner." "Sure, Mom, as soon as Bart Simpson is over. Don't worry, I'll take care of it." About an hour later, Mom can be heard shrieking at the top of her lungs, "Barry, that dog has barbecue sauce smeared all over my clean, white kitchen floor! I thought you said you were going to take the garbage out! Why can't you ever do what you say you are going to do?" Sheepishly comes the all too familiar reply, "Sorry, Mom, I guess I forgot." Barry's selective memory strikes again.

Lindsay's temper had a hidden cost that perpetuated the anger cycle. She was so formidable, so frightening, that Barry felt powerless in the face of her fury. Lacking a direct method of problem solving with Mom at this point, he devised an indirect system of payback. This spirited "chip off the old block" fought back silently.

If your child's memory is giving you an ulcer, it may be his or her version of passive warfare. Kids sometimes get off by getting your goat. They seem to get a perverse kind of emotional satisfaction out of making you mad. Think about it: How else can a child get back at his or her parents? Older children punish their parents by making them mad or by making them worry. Babies, toddlers, and preschoolers *never* punish parents. As long as children continue to believe in Santa Claus or the Easter Bunny, they are not capable of punishing parents at all. As they become better able to distinguish fantasy and reality, they can and frequently do decide to manipulate you. Some kids are experts at driving you crazy with passive aggression. But passive warfare is a lose-lose situation. You lose because you feel like a failure as a parent. Your child loses because, increasingly, the child comes to think of himself or herself as a bad person.

You simply don't have to continue living this way. As you get a better understanding of yourself, you will be better equipped to duck those emotional sucker punches. You will learn to see them coming in advance. Your improved peripheral vision will enable you to recognize the arousal of angry thoughts and angry emotions *before* they lead you to hostile behavior, passive or otherwise. You will also learn a set of research-proven actions to help you to reframe hostile trigger thoughts that accelerate angry thoughts and feelings. This will increase positive exchanges among loved ones.

But have no doubt about it, if you are caring for an impulsive or otherwise challenging youngster, your load is not going to be an easy one to bear. You will be angry many times. You need to learn to anticipate these angry thoughts as well as the feelings they trigger. By anticipating them, you will not be developing a self-fulfilling prophecy or negative mind-set. You will be developing a realistic appraisal of what you can and cannot do to improve your relationship with your child.

In this book I frequently refer to the hyperactive child, but most parents have their hands full with so-called "normal" children. Kimberley is just such a mom. Kimberley does not have a hyperactive child. But Jason, her middle child, had a knack for bringing out the worst in her. It seemed as if Jason lived to embarrass his mother. On the way home from a day at the beach Kimberley was too hot and tired to cook dinner. Besides, she thought the kids would enjoy eating at McDonald's. The group settled down, and Kimberley had just taken a bite of her Big Mac when Jason bellowed, "Mom, you know I hate cheese on my burger. How many times do I have to tell you that? I'm not going to eat this crap." Kimberley felt mortified, her meal ruined. But what could she do? There was Jason's friend, Bart, to think about. She also had to struggle hard to resist the urge to reach around and pinch Jason's ears off.

Instead of smacking Jason, she thought about the C.O.O.L. Rules:

C—Consider the context and consequences of my reactions to provocative situations that trigger my anger.

O—Observe my breathing, body tension, and communication objectively.

O—Organize options for successful problem solving when provoked.

L—Look to the future, learn from the past and live in the present.

Kimberley remembered a tool she is currently trying to get comfortable with: goal setting. Goal setting is one tool she is determined to master. Kimberley has begun setting goals for *her* behavior when she is provoked by her son in public. Easier said than done? You bet. But she now realizes if she is ever going to stop Jason's public misbehavior, she must first stop his perverse payoff. Weird as it seemed at first, it is now becoming obvious that her anger is his payoff.

Kimberley is learning to reflect *before* she reacts in anger. Let's look at how she used the C.O.O.L. Rules in this situation. She

Considered the context and consequences.
    She is hot, tired, dehydrated, and hungry. The kids are also. Jason is impulsive, a bit spoiled, and prone to using rude challenges to impress his friends.

Trigger behavior:

> Jason's rude remark: "Mom, you know I hate cheese on my burger. How many times do I have to tell you that? I'm not going to eat this crap."

Trigger thought:

> Kimberley's thought: "You disrespectful little brat, I ought to slap your face."

Observed herself objectively.

> Breathing is shallow and rapid.
> Body tension is high.
> Self-talk is accelerating her anger.
> Feels mortified, violated, and angry.

Organized Options.

1. Belly breathe.
2. Melt muscle tension.
3. Look to the future. Communicate constructive, calming thoughts to self:
   1. "I see myself calmly speaking to Jason as I finish my drink."
   2. Exchange trigger thought for C.O.O.L. thought: "Showing my anger will increase Jason's rude behavior in the future. I know how to handle this situation. I need to communicate calmly to Jason."

> Then Action: "Your language is rude and unacceptable. You may choose to eat the burger or leave it. But this is supper. There will be no more to eat until breakfast. I will receive an apology by the time we leave this table or you will not be included the next time we go out to eat."

If Jason apologizes immediately, Kimberley may regain her appetite and forget the incident ever happened. If Jason continues to be rude, she will take him immediately to the car (if it is safe to do so), saying no more to him. She will instruct the others to finish their meal while she takes Jason to the car. Or tell them to pick up their food and finish it in the car on the way home. Part of Jason's punishment will be to clean up any crumbs left in the car.

Kimberley considered the C.O.O.L. Rules. She considered the context and consequences, observed her reactions objectively, organized her options. She looked to the future with optimism, while learning from the past and living in the present. *Before* Kimberley got to the restaurant she planned ahead. In her mind she saw herself at the table with Jason. The food had barely arrived when he started acting up. In her mind's eye she saw herself in total control of the situation. She even had a plan to reward or punish Jason in a calm, controlled manner when they got back home. Does she still get caught off guard occasionally? Of course, but the plan provides a form of security, a systematic method to evaluate both herself and Jason. She can gauge her level of progress based on how well she is working the plan. She can change the plan in a systematic manner as necessary. Somewhere along the way, she has lost that Chicken Little blend of panic, helplessness, and despair she used to experience when she sensed that she was failing as a mother. She feels more adequate and successful in her role now. It reassures her to know that she needs only look up to prove to herself that the sky is, indeed, still in its proper location.

You, like Kimberley, may get angry too often with your child. Like Jason, your child may be a handful even though he or she is not hyperactive. If so, commit yourself to fight negative thoughts that trigger feelings of anger, shame, or embarrassment. You can be the parent you want to be. Too much of the time you may simply "lose it" because you lack the skills to do otherwise. You really can find a better way. Many of us say or do those ineffective self-esteem destroyers that hurt our children. If you have been feeling guilty and you keep hearing yourself saying, "I must be a rotten parent if my child is not hyperactive and I still can't stop screaming, right?" answer quickly and assertively, "Wrong!" Nothing could be further from the truth!

The reason for talking about the hyperactive child is simple. The hyperactive child is probably the most provocative and challenging of all children. The hyperactive child can push any parent's hot button. The hyperactive child is chosen as an example to represent the ultimate challenge to any adult's patience. In my twenty-odd years as a psychologist to adults, families, teens, and children, I have come to realize that the very techniques that help parents tame their tempers with the most provocative of offspring should be shared with all adults who care for children. Because sooner or later, if you care for children, your patience will be tested.

Parenting is a lot like coaching an athlete. All coaches want success for their teams. They spend endless hours preparing to win, but coaches know they won't win all the time. After the game, win or lose, coach and players must pull together in preparation for the next game.

Remember, your goal is not to "win" every contest with your child. Your goal is to raise a happy, productive, responsible adult. In the pages that follow, you will learn how to use the tools that will help you reach that goal. My hope is that you and your children will be victorious over the forces of society placing today's youngsters at great risk of falling prey to virtually all of society's ills.

Consider the long-term point of view; lifestyle changes are what is needed. Quick fixes don't work. Remember, it is okay to be angry; anger is simply an emotion. It is hostile behavior that makes anger a destructive force. You are already learning guidelines you will need to prevent your anger from becoming hostility. But guidelines are not infallible. When you fail, and there will be times when you fail, pick yourself up and start over again. The worst thing you can do is to allow the domino theory of anger management to take effect. In the domino theory, people say, "I screwed up, I give up, what difference does it make anyway?" Believe me, it makes all the difference in the world. When it comes to child rearing, it's not whether you win or lose every little engagement. How you play the game of life is what really counts.

When you learn to control your behavior, your child will come to view you as an individual who is trying to cope with overpowering emotions. Your child's observations of you will eventually lead him or her to imitate and emulate your attempts to manage your surging emotions before they overflow their banks and destroy your home. The simple fact of attempting to cope, and of learning and trying to grow, is a positive role model. Obviously, we would all like to be successful all of the time. Equally obviously, we will fail some of the time. Give it your best shot and when you don't make it, regroup, reevaluate, and try again. In time, your children will learn to cope with the high energy that compels them to impulsive, annoying, frightening, and self-defeating actions.

CHAPTER 3

The Power of Learning

Consider the following scene: You're sitting at the kitchen table making out the grocery list. Suddenly a *crash!* and screams emanate from the TV room.

As an un-C.O.O.L. parent, you might run into the TV room screaming, "What's going on here?!" "What are you (BLANK) kids up to now?" "What the (BLANK) got broken this time?" and other such intelligent and well-thought-out comments. Or you might say something else equally ineffective like "Now you've done it! Just wait till your father gets home. You'll really get it then!"

Then, at the height of your un-C.O.O.L.ness, the following actions unfold:

YELL,
YANK,
SPANK,
FEEL GUILTY LATER.

If it was an older child you unloaded all your wrath on, screaming, yelling, and beating, maybe that child got to the telephone and called the Child Abuse Hotline. And you got investigated. No more! You are learning to be a C.O.O.L. parent, to take control of your own life. You are ready to respond effectively; with loving concern, moderation of anger, and no guilt rebound. Many parenting systems ask you to be unemotional. But as a C.O.O.L. parent there will be plenty of emotion in what you do, positive emotion! Love, a sense of mastery, a sense of yourself as a successful parent! Guess what? Your child will feel it, too! Love is contagious. Love is generative. That cycle of anger and guilt that springs from lack of patience, angry retort, and excessive punishment will become a thing of the past. As a C.O.O.L. parent, you know what to do when a "situation" arises— use your C.O.O.L. skills. To repeat:

C—Consider the context and consequences of your reactions to provocative situations;

O—Observe your breathing, body tension, and communication objectively;

O—Organize your options for problem solving;

L—Look to the future while learning from the past and living in the present.

You'll be planning to respond effectively *before* the situation occurs. Think of it as a form of mental training much like that used by our Olympic athletes. As C.O.O.L. parents you will benefit by being equipped with the tools of the parenting trade. We always try to equip our children with the skills they will need to be successful adults, to teach them desirable habits, skills, morals, and values while minimizing the development of undesirable habits, skills, or abilities. Of course we aren't responsible for everything our youngsters learn, good or bad. It's almost frightening to learn how early in their lives our children begin to pick up mannerisms, words, and behavior from other children, other members of the family, even people they see on TV. Children ages two to five spend an average of about 25 hours per week exposed to TV. For older children the number is only slightly less. This TV time exposes them to 250,000 acts of violence and 40,000 attempted murders by age eighteen. Violence on TV and in movies does lead to aggressive behavior with siblings and others, according to the National Institute of Mental Health and the American Academy of Pediatrics.

And yet the end of family fellowship and unrelenting media attacks on traditional values are far more destructive than TV violence. As the cultural experiment with our minds continues to replace common sense with trendy social theory fresh from the school of "what's happening now," parents and children suffer. As children and adults strive to emulate their newly defined heroes, the emphasis on rights, and deemphasis on personal responsibility, continues to produce social erosion on a grand scale, which you experience as rebellion on a smaller scale at home. About the best you can do then is to increase the probability of behaviors that you consider healthy, and decrease the probability of behaviors that you view as dangerous, destructive, or unhealthy. How do you do this? Here's how: Behavior patterns are either instinctive or learned, right? We have little control over behavior that is acquired instinctively. The genetic blueprints for instinct are laid down at the moment of conception. But we do have control over behavior patterns that are learned.

Fortunately, a lot of our behavior is learned, and behavior that is learned or instinctive can be influenced in the following ways. *Observation:* Observing others and imitating what we see them doing. *Association:* This is what is known as Pavlovian "conditioned" learning, associating a particular emotion, thought, or behavior with a particular stimulus. Many emotional responses are learned by association. *Consequences:* Behavior that is reinforced will increase. Behavior that is punished will decrease. *Rules:* Behavior based on rules can be acquired by hearing an explanation of the relationship involved. Consider the example of a traffic light. We stop when the light is red simply because it is red and we have learned the significance of the rule "Stop on red."

As C.O.O.L. parents, you're covering the observational part. Your child will have a good role model for behaving rationally in a tense situation. Because you are more in control of yourself, you are setting a good example, reinforcing the desirability of such good behavior for your child. This will, of course, make it possible for your child to feel more positive about his or her own good behavior, because your child sees it as coming from you. You now know how to manage your emotions in difficult situations. You're also a good role model because you *think before you act*, and you manage anger more effectively than you used to. Let's look at an example.

Tony, who had been practicing the C.O.O.L. techniques, was pleasantly surprised when he noticed that his fourteen-year-old son, Carl, was beginning to follow his lead by dealing with his own disappointments in a more mature manner, especially regarding his adventuresome friend named Barry. Barry, of selective memory fame, was the type of kid who would come up with pretty wild ideas about how to have a good time. One night, about two weeks before Halloween, Tony got the call from the police station after the boys had been arrested driving Tony's car. It seemed that the boys had been parked down the street from Barry's house, talking, when the squad car arrived. Officer Robinson was making the rounds through the neighborhood at the time, and neither boy could produce a valid driver's license when asked to identify himself. Carl had gotten real nervous and told the officer that this was his father's car. It seemed that Barry and Carl figured no one would be the wiser if they snuck the car out and took it for a spin after Tony fell asleep. The plan would have worked if Officer Robinson hadn't wandered by when he did. He brought the boys home after putting the fear of God in them.

For months before this incident, Carl had been very moody. Angry exchanges between him and his father had become a daily thing. Tony was worried about Carl's temper. It was bad enough when he had to confront Carl for lying or forgetting to straighten up his room, but some of the language coming out of Carl's room during his phone fights with his girlfriend seemed way out of bounds from Tony's point of view. He decided to practice the C.O.O.L. techniques in an effort to deal with Carl's unruly behavior.

Almost two months had gone by since he started making a conscious effort to keep his C.O.O.L. Now to his relief and astonishment he noticed that Carl was taking on the role of counselor to some of his friends. On the phone he could hear Carl telling Barry, "Don't do it! Is it worth it? Take a deep breath, calm down, you better consider the consequences!" Was this really Tony's kid giving Barry advice on how to get along better with his mother? Now that was a switch.

Maybe there really is something to this role model business. In fact, Tony had become a good role model in a whole range of areas. Carl still had a way to go, but he did seem to be going in the right direction.

Associational learning was also coming into play now. Carl was learning to associate his misbehavior with calm, consistent, firm behavior on Tony's part. Tony even referred to Carl's screwups as mistakes. Carl could now associate his mistakes with opportunities for informative instruction and corrective action rather than hysterical ranting. Carl and Tony talked more about options, and because so much emphasis was placed on making choices, Carl was more willing to speak up and try to "cut a deal" before, rather than after, the damage had been done. He could live with the consequences of his choices because he felt more responsibility for selecting the options he chose. I guess you could say Carl didn't need to fight his father for respect so often now that he could feel that he had it.

Consequential is another type of learning. By this, I mean learning that is controlled by consequences that follow it.

Consider how you learned to drive a car. You put the car in drive. When you pushed the gas pedal, you discovered that the car moved forward. The consequences of not learning this simple rule are rapid and dangerous! It usually takes only one time to learn what happens when you push the gas pedal. But what if the gas pedal were disconnected? You might press the pedal one or two times, expecting the car to move. But if the pressing behavior were not reinforced the way you had come to expect it to be—with the movement of the car—you would soon stop pressing the pedal. You learned to press the pedal because as a consequence of pressing, the car moved. You would learn to stop pressing the pedal if the car quit moving. Much behavior is learned the same way. If it is reinforced by the consequences, it will continue. If good behavior is ignored, one of two things will become immediately apparent. If the behavior had been reinforced on a very regular basis and the reinforcement stops, you might initially see a lot of very agitated behavior of the type that had previously been reinforced. This would be an effort to reestablish the reinforcement. Or soon the good behavior would stop when it was no longer reinforced.

This would be very similar to you going up to the soft drink machine where you work. If it had always filled your order, you would certainly expect it to do so each time you inserted the money. But let's suppose that after several years of working flawlessly, the machine does not produce a drink. Depending on how thirsty you are, you might tap on it a few times or you might put more money in. If the machine did not give you a drink this time and you were very thirsty, you would probably not put any more money in it but would instead go somewhere else for a drink.

If, however, you worked in a location where the soft drink machine didn't work on a regular basis, but occasionally did work if you gave it a good, firm tap, you might find yourself banging on the machine any morning it didn't deliver. If you were very thirsty in this case, you might continue putting money in and banging on the machine, especially if your office had a policy of reimbursing you for money lost this way. Sometimes behavior that has been very well established on an inconsistent schedule of reinforcement will be more persistent when the reinforcement stops. Other times, when the reinforcement has been more consistent, when it stops, the behavior will stop.

So, if you have, unwittingly, been reinforcing your child's misbehavior through negative attention, it will be more resistant to change. If you have been doing a lot of ranting and raving in much the same way Danielle had been doing with eight-year-old Allie, your child, like Allie, has probably learned to ignore you until she can almost feel your hands on her buttocks. Allie had learned that she did not have to respond to her mother's requests for her to stop. She needed only to respond when she could see the red of her mother's eyes. It is important to remember as we go through these exercises that when you make the choice to C.O.O.L. down and respond in a more reasonable way, such as Tony is now doing with his son, you are also reinforcing your child's correct behavior of listening to you. Because of Carl's age, the need to feel respected was very important to him. Respect was a very powerful reinforcer and one that he worked hard to continue receiving. He liked and responded well to that consequence. Carl also responded well to the association of the positive feelings he felt when he was closer with his father. These feelings were not necessarily direct consequences of something his father was doing to make Carl feel better. Rather, the sense of closeness that he felt was associated with Carl's compliance to reasonable requests and with paying attention.

If your child has become used to seeing you react with anger, screaming and yelling whenever he or she misbehaves, and you no longer do that, your child sees a change. When your child becomes convinced that his or her misbehavior doesn't cause your motor to race anymore, you will have arrived at the threshold of the Promised Land. Your children will start to be more amenable to what you have to say. They will begin to listen more often and begin to anticipate and respect the consequences of their choices *before* they have to experience them. Once you, or someone like Officer Robinson, get their attention, the rules that connect choices to consequences may not be popular but they will be considered. That wonderful place in a parent and child's relationship where mature logic, rationality, and rule-governed behavior become commonplace will seem much closer.

When thinking about rule-governed learning, remember the traffic light analogy. The light turns green, you go; when it's yellow, you exercise caution; if it is red, you stop. You don't have to be involved in several crashes before you understand the rule. The information that explains the relationship between the choice and the consequence becomes known to us, we accept it, and behave accordingly.

A large part of our behavior is rule-governed. In most cases and for most people this is automatic. But challenging children have a hard time learning to use rules! ADHD kids are so impulsive, they forget the rules they know at the time they most need to apply them. That's one major reason that they annoy so many people. That's also why nagging and lectures don't work. Lectures are explanations of rules. Nagging is repetitious lecturing. Scolding is another form of telling the rules—or should I say "yelling" the rules? Kids don't listen well. Unless they're interested, they simply tune out. So what should you do? Speak softly and carry a big stick? No. Speak as little as possible and follow through a lot!

At first, you apply these techniques on faith because you haven't done things just this way before. But once you experience success and realize that these techniques do work, your efforts will be reinforced by positive results.

CHAPTER 4

Headaches, Backaches, and Stressful Situations

Headaches, backaches, and even upset stomachs are frequently caused by tension. It does not take a lot of tension to make you ache. Try this simple experiment, to convince yourself just how closely the mind and body work together. Ask yourself, "How does my right arm feel at this very moment?" "What sensations am I experiencing in my right arm?" Pay particular attention to the area between the elbow and the wrist. What are you sensing in that part of your arm that tells you that it is distinct, separate from the rest of the limb? If I were a betting man, I might wager that you don't know how it feels, because you do not normally pay very close attention to how your right arm feels.

Now pick up this book in your right hand and hold it at arm's length for sixty seconds. After thirty seconds, probably sooner, you will begin to be aware of how your right arm feels. You will feel the tension in your arm. When you do, put the book down. If you held your arm out there long enough, that little bit of tension would actually create some soreness in your right arm while your left arm would feel fine.

Now imagine how you would feel if you hung on to that tension every day. It takes very little tension to lead to muscle strain and physical discomfort. Many of us feel tension in our shoulders first, near the base of the neck, or in our stomachs. But headaches are probably the most common source of pain due to stress. If you experience frequent headaches, you may be storing low-level muscle tension across your forehead. The temple region is another tension spot for many headache victims. But the granddaddy of all tension

29

spots is the jaw. Many parents, particularly yellers and screamers, carry a lot of tension in their jaws.

The rage that you feel when you're angry at your children also causes physical pain. Even the Arthritis Foundation now acknowledges this mind/body relationship. In their literature, they discuss how to reduce the discomfort of arthritic pain by reducing the level of tension and stress in your life.

Pain also affects our dispositions. It makes us nasty. Since you are working so hard to become a C.O.O.L. parent and improve your disposition, it just makes good sense to minimize pain and discomfort when you can. You will feel a lot better if you simply learn to scan your body for tension. When you recognize that your forehead, temple, or jaw is tense, smile and let go of the tension. When you feel tension mounting, turn it loose. It feels so good. Let your whole face, jaw, neck, and shoulders go rag-doll limp. Consider the life of a piece of pasta. Before it is cooked, the pasta is rigid, so rigid, in fact, that it is brittle. Consider what happens to that piece of pasta when it's cooked. The pasta absorbs water and becomes flexible. It becomes so bendable, it rolls easily up on your fork ready to enjoy.

As you consider strategies for keeping C.O.O.L., remember the pasta. You, like the pasta, will learn to become more flexible, to adapt. This doesn't mean you will have to give in to your child's every whim. When you see trouble coming, prepare your mind and body for the fray that is certain to follow. First, scan your jaw, shoulders, and neck to let go of the early signs of tension. The sooner you do this, the easier it is to let tension go.

Kevin and his wife Sara get plenty of practice with scanning and releasing muscle tension. Aaron, their eleven-year-old son, sees to that. Aaron can be the most lovable and affectionate of children. But Aaron has a secret. Aaron is a world-class consistency checker. And just what does a consistency checker do? He checks parental consistency, that's what. Aaron never misses an opportunity to exploit a difference between his parents. If Sarah and Kevin disagree on anything of importance to an eleven-year-old, Aaron will find a way to turn that difference to his advantage. A recent controversy over an R-rated video provided a case in point.

Aaron and Kevin are browsing through the selections at the video store when Aaron proudly announces that he is able to secure the only remaining copy of the new movie *Dracula*. Kevin feels the base of his neck start to tighten as his explanations of why the movie is not appropriate are drowned out by Aaron's increasingly louder insistence that "Mom said I could see it. Mom said *she* went to Dracula movies when she was my age, Dad." Kevin and his wife have not discussed this particular movie. He is positively opposed to Aaron watching explicit sex and violence. Sarah is a bit more permissive, but Kevin is quite sure that Sarah is not ready for her son to be entertained by modern R-rated versions of the legend of Count Dracula. As the pleading turns to demanding, Kevin is reminded of how he would have handled this situation a few months ago. Now, instead of boiling, threatening, or yelling, as he used to do, Kevin stretches, shrugs his shoulders, and enjoys the pleasant sensations of tense muscles letting go. He takes a few deep breaths and walks to the men's room to buy some time and gather his thoughts. When he returns, he selects a movie he's sure the rest of the family will enjoy and Aaron is informed that his behavior is inappropriate, and that he will have to wait until next week to make the movie selection.

Aaron didn't like it, but the ensuing temper tantrum lasted only two minutes. On the drive home, Kevin continued to scan and release the tension that sprouted between his shoulder blades. He also reminded himself of just how much quicker Aaron settles down, now that Dad has begun to stretch instead of shout. The discussion with Sarah about how best to compromise on their differences over appropriate movies also went a lot smoother. In the old days, he and Sarah would have had a big row over that one for sure.

Children need discipline; they thrive on firmness. But firmness and fuming make for an unhappy family. Firmness plus a plan for dealing with unexpected stress you most certainly will encounter is the best solution. In chapter 7, we will consider the importance of rehearsing and the significance of developing a practice plan. After a few practice sessions, you will be ready to put yourself and your tools to work.

Kevin said it best: "Recognizing and releasing muscle tension is a bit like swimming. When I swim, I start with one stroke, but I do not stop there or I will surely sink. When I swim, I take one stroke, then another, and eventually I develop a rhythm—stroking, then gliding, then stroking some more. Recognizing and releasing muscle tension requires a rhythm as well. When I'm swimming a short distance, only a few strokes are needed, but if I must swim a long way or swim in rough water, more strokes will be needed. When I am very irritable, a lot of scanning and releasing is required to keep me cool."

Children will wear you out. They have more energy than you. You must be prepared to pace yourself. A C.O.O.L. parent develops a library of alternative solutions to problems and uses them. You will also require flexibility and ingenuity in applying these alternatives. If you are too rigid, you, like the dry pasta, will break under the many demands your kids will place upon you. Don't forget, these children will be with you for a long, long time. By learning to step aside from anger, you, your spouse, and your children will be happier, and will esteem yourselves more.

Remember the Boy Scout motto and be prepared. Parents must be aware in order to be prepared. By being aware, you will avoid getting blindsided by anger. Stress from any source will make you more vulnerable to the hothead. You might even say that when your plate gets too full, your feelings get foul.

Ask Lindsay about the full plate problem. "Full? Heck, my plate is spilling over. I have got to find a way to simplify my life." If Lindsay's thoughts sound like something you may have been thinking lately, join the club. From my vantage point, Lindsay's thoughts are shared by a lot more people every day. I'm sure you're already aware that your life is filled with a number of stress-producing factors other than your child. Money is tight for everyone these days. World events, social problems, and the state of the environment concern most of us.

What about your work? If you still have a job, is being asked to do more with less, or other job stressors, making it harder for you to keep your C.O.O.L.? Stress tolerance has become the new badge of courage in Lindsay's office. How much pressure you are handling is now considered the litmus test for a quality employee. Are you in a stressful personal relationship? How's your health? And the health of your loved ones? These and other factors influence your sense of well-being and your sense of adequacy as a person and a parent, and are part of the context of your daily interactions with your children. The state of the world economy and global ecology are pretty much outside your control. But marital and work stress are things you may be able to do something about.

Working with a therapist may help your marriage. If you think you have been overlooked for promotion, maybe you need to have a conference with your boss. If your budget has got the better of you, consumer credit counseling can help. My recommendation is that you do whatever you can to improve the overall condition of your life. You will then be better prepared to deal with your children on more even terms.

In the next few pages, you are going to learn how to identify, label, and rate specific, *predictable* stress-producing situations that occur between you and your child. These techniques are also helpful for flash anger, but we will consider other techniques for that as well. Later, you will also learn to track your emotional needs and stresses, as well as your personal arousal level. An increase in your body's physiological tension level always accompanies psychological tension. Psychological tension is caused by ignoring or inadequately nourishing your emotional needs as well as by stressors from the outside. Any combination of the above may be the culprit when it comes to increasing your susceptibility to anger triggers. Arousal is a close relative to tension. It almost always precedes anger, hostility, or aggression.

Arousal is also known as the fight-or-flight response. The term *fight-or-flight* is a throwback to the days when a human's main stress revolved around the daily struggle to determine whether he or she would eat, or be lunch that day. In the movie *Jurassic Park*, as in the days of the dinosaurs, the struggle to survive required high levels of readiness when the danger signal sounded. Today, stress sets off the danger signals. Our bodies get physically prepared for a fight to the death or a race for our life when we are tense, upset, or startled. Arousal is frequently evidenced by the quickening of our pulse. The alarm is internal. A state of readiness is declared by our hormone system. As your body declares ever higher states of alert, more hormones find their way to your bloodstream. Angry people hear the sounds of too many false alarms. Too often the angry adult leaps before he or she looks. Those of us in need of temper taming go, too quickly and too often, from a state of alert to a state of action, or more correctly overreaction, and, far too commonly, aggression. High levels of tension and arousal make it too easy to fly off the handle.

The Situation Barometer and Personal Arousal Thermometer

To help you identify, measure, and manage your tension and arousal levels, I would like to introduce you to a couple of tools from the

C.O.O.L. toolbox for parents: the Situation Barometer and the Personal Arousal Thermometer. First, the Barometer. It is designed to help you to consider the context in which you lose your temper. Appraising the context of your most Forgettable Flare-ups is the first step.

Assume that a tension-causing situation is approaching, the type of situation that frequently precedes an ugly encounter with your child. Maybe it's time for the school bus to arrive. Any moment now little Lacy is sure to come flying through the front door. It's been raining for a week but somehow she can't seem to remember to leave her muddy shoes in the mud room. Or, perhaps, you are coming home from work and preparing to face the baby-sitter. You know the kinds of situations I'm talking about!

On the following page you'll find a Situation Barometer Work Sheet. Take several minutes now to identify and rate different situations for their ability to trigger your anger. There are no right and wrong answers, because everyone's high and low anger triggers will differ. So just follow along and you'll begin to see how it works.

List some of the most common tension/anger-producing situations you face regularly with your child. Jot them down, with no particular order in mind. Include situations that never fail to make you angry.

Next, look over your list and give each situation an anger rating. Rate these events on a scale of 1 to 10. Let's think here in terms similar to the ratings the National Weather Service uses when they're tracking storms out in the Atlantic that might turn into hurricanes. My definitions are a little different, but the idea is the same:

- Class 1 (0–2) is a mild day. Maybe a little windy, but nothing you can't handle. Everything's okay. I call this a low anger situation. No problem.
- Class 2 (3–4) is windy with a little rain. But the rain probably won't last long enough to become too much of a bother. This is an inconvenience, but only a mild disturbance.
- Class 3 (5–7) weather is getting pretty rough. High winds, lots of heavy rain. Time to seek shelter. It's going to be a rough night! Moderate disturbance.
- Class 4 (8–9) is a full-blown tropical storm with damaging winds, torrential rain, and roofs being blown off houses. Very

significant disturbance.
- Class 5 (10+) is Hurricane "_____." Total destruction! This monster comes crashing ashore and everything in its path is flattened. If you want to put your child's or spouse's name in the blank space, go right ahead. Maximum disturbance.
- Now close your eyes for a minute or so and imagine the most relaxed, calm, and peaceful experience you can ever remember having. Give that a rating of Class 0.

SITUATION BAROMETER

List below situations that regularly contribute to your anger. Rate each of them based on their potential to produce anger.

1. _____

_____

2. _____

_____

3. _____

_____

4. _____

_____

5. _____

_____

Go back now and color in the details of each scene. Identify and include mitigating circumstances that increase your potential to pop off at loved ones. These might include such things as work stress, fatigue, lack of sex, use of alcohol and drugs, pain, hunger, or other pressures.

RATING SCALE

1 — Mild	0–2
2 — Windy but bearable	3–4
3 — Blustery, use caution	5–7
4 — Storm	8–9
5 — Hurricane!	10+

Your Situation Barometer helps you identify and measure the stress you feel in certain situations. And, just like the weather, it will change from day to day. Most important, you can use the barometer technique to help you analyze the context of potentially troublesome situations. The whole point is to look at a situation before it occurs. Identify its potential to make you mad and plan to handle that situation better than in the past. You've probably included one particular situation on your barometer, one that never fails to yank your chain. Use that situation to illustrate how the next step in the process—objectively observing your breathing, body tension, and communication—is related to your anger.

This process is like taking what we might call your "Personal Arousal TEMPERature" using the "Thermometer" I've included below.

PERSONAL AROUSAL THERMOMETER

96°–98°	This is the Action Zone.
Breathing:	Rhythmic, regular
Muscle Tension:	Relaxed
Communication:	Self-talk—"That's nice. I can handle this."
Voice Quality:	Volume moderate, message affirming/neutral
Gaze:	Soft eyes inviting approach of any type
Movement:	Smooth, controlled, in your own space
Feeling:	Happy, comfortable, complete sense of self-control

You feel calm and collected. You can accept criticism. You can listen to an unpopular opinion. You have full confidence in your ability to responsibly handle anything you hear. You feel safe and spontaneous. You have a high tolerance. Go ahead and act!

99°–100°	*Not So Fast!*
Breathing:	Quickening
Muscle Tension:	Slight increase—moderate
Communication:	Self-talk—"What is she thinking?" "Where is he coming from?"
Voice Quality:	Volume moderate, message questioning/complaining
Gaze:	Quizzical, more intense
Movement:	Controlled, gesturing in own space
Feeling:	Alert/puzzled, adequate self-control

Pause. Consider context cues and identify trigger thoughts. Observe yourself closely. Scan your body. If you feel tension increasing: belly breathe, melt muscle tension, communicate with affirming, calming self-talk, body language, and words. Organize—plan your actions. Look to the future. See yourself interacting calmly with your child. Your actions are tempered by memories of your Success Stories and Forgettable Flare-ups. Consider chilling out by taking a break if necessary. Act only when you feel that you are in the Action Zone.

101°–102°	*Stop*
Breathing:	Rapid, shallow
Muscle Tension:	High
Communication:	Self-talk—"It's all your fault!" "He always does the dumbest things. What will he he think of next?" "Get lost!"
Voice Quality:	Volume moderately loud/flat, message confrontational/blaming, overgeneralizing, critical, demeaning, dismissing
Gaze:	Looking away or staring intently
Movement:	Quicker; gesturing, moving, or leaning closer into child's space
Feeling:	Irritated/moderately angry, reasonable self-control

Pause. You feel anger accelerating. Consider context cues and identify trigger thoughts. Observe yourself closely. Scan your body. If you feel tension increasing: belly breathe, melt muscle tension, communicate with affirming, calming self-talk, body language, and words. Organize—plan your actions. Look to the future. See yourself interacting calmly with your child. Your actions are tempered by memories of your Success Stories and Forgettable Flare-ups. Chill Out—take a break. Visualize yourself being effective. Wait until your TEMPERature has returned to Action Zone before taking action. Act only when you feel that you are in the Action Zone.

103°–104°	*Get Out of There!*
Breathing:	Rapid, shallow
Muscle tension:	Rigid, set
Communication:	Self-talk—totally negative, all or none. "Get out of here or else." "He really is stupid. He's trying to drive me crazy. This situation is hopeless."
Voice Quality:	Volume loud, message threatening/insulting, demeaning/accusing, mind reading/arbitrary/overgeneralizing
Gaze:	Intense and piercing
Movement:	Rapid, in child's space
Feeling:	High anger, doubtful self-control

Back off. Your behavior is highly provocative. You are sending signals that say, "Submit now or defend yourself now." Ask yourself, "Is this the message I intend?"

You feel anger accelerating. Consider context cues and identify trigger thoughts. Observe yourself closely. Scan your body. As you feel tension increasing: belly breathe, melt muscle tension, communicate with affirming, calming self-talk, body language, and words. Organize—plan your actions. Look to the future. See yourself interacting calmly with your child. Your actions are tempered by memories of your Success Stories and Forgettable Flare-ups. Chill Out—take a break. Visualize yourself being effective. Wait until your TEMPERature has returned to the Action Zone before taking action. Act only when you feel that you are in the Action Zone.

105°+	*Don't Touch It with a 10-Foot Pole!*
Breathing:	Rapid, shallow
Muscle tension:	Rigid, set
Communication:	Self-talk—hostile, attacking."I'm going to kick your butt." "I ought to beat you to within an inch of your life."
Voice Quality:	Volume screaming, message humiliation, profanity, global labels, "You are under attack, surrender/fight/flee."
Gaze:	Wild-eyed or intensely focused
Movement:	Agitated, striking out physically
Feeling:	Hate/contempt, tenuous self-control

Leave the area immediately after securing the safety of your child. You are out of control! The probability of violence is extremely high. Dispute your negative self-talk. Call a friend. Count to a thousand. Move slowly. Speak softly. Do not attempt discipline, reasoning, or any type of interaction with your child. As you leave, pay close attention to your self-talk and follow the steps outlined below:

Consider context cues and identify trigger thoughts. Observe yourself closely. Scan your body. If you feel tension increasing: belly breathe, melt muscle tension, communicate with affirming, calming self-talk, body language, and words. Organize—plan your actions. Look to the future. See yourself interacting calmly with your child. Your actions are tempered by memories of your Success Stories and Forgettable Flare-ups. Chill Out—take a break. Visualize yourself being effective. Wait until your TEMPERature has returned to the Action Zone before taking action. Act only when you feel that you are in the Action Zone.

Now that you know how to take your temperature, let's move to organizing your options. Organizing options is dependent upon the accuracy of your observations and your ability to make healthy choices. We know that unhealthy anger both creates and is created by distorted thinking. That is why considering context triggers, consequences, breathing, muscle relaxation, and communication are so important. Timing is also very important. Dr. Gerald Paterson and his colleagues at the Oregon Social Learning Center have been scientifically studying anger escalation patterns for more than twenty years. They have discovered that the likelihood of violence increases significantly when angry verbal exchanges that contain certain trigger behaviors continue for over thirty seconds. I know that this seems like a very short time, but most angry exchanges involve only two or three comments hurled back and forth very quickly. When the verbal barrage continues beyond this point, the likelihood of violence increases dramatically.

Remember the old adage "Practice makes perfect." The more you practice C.O.O.L. skills, the sooner they will become a part of your personality.

Once you've assessed the situation and your personal arousal level, you can complete the analytical process. I'm going to describe the process for you below. Then you can work through the steps on your own using the work sheet pages that follow:

1. Close your eyes.
2. Replay the troublesome scene on your brain's TV monitor. Don't spend more than a minute or two doing this.
3. Write down the thoughts you were having during the scene and ask yourself, "Did these thoughts help me deal with the situation? Did they hurt?"
4. Now assess the feelings you were having. And ask yourself, "Did these feelings help? Did they hurt?"
5. Now what about the action you took? Write down what you did. Did it help, or did it hurt?

Analysis Work Sheet #1

Describe the scene briefly:

_____

_____

_____

Your thoughts: *helpful/hurtful*

_____

_____

_____

Your feelings: *helpful/hurtful*

_____

_____

_____

Your action: *helpful/hurtful*

_____

_____

_____

ANALYSIS WORK SHEET #2

Now think about what you could have done differently. Follow the same steps as before: Close your eyes and replay the scene in your mind. But this time—using the work sheet—write down what you could have thought, what you could have felt, action you could have taken that might have improved the outcome.

Describe the scene briefly:

_____

_____

_____

What you could have thought:

_____

_____

_____

What you could have felt:

_____

_____

_____

How you might have acted differently:

_____

_____

_____

Don't be too concerned if you had fewer "could haves" than you might have hoped. A large portion of the rest of this book will be spent discussing ways to change your behavior, ways you and your child might behave in troublesome situations in the future. Your success rate will get better. You will become a more effective parent. Later on, you should return to these work sheet pages to see how much you've learned.

You may have heard or read Reinhold Neibuhr's famous "Serenity Prayer": "God, grant me the Serenity to accept the things I cannot change, the Courage to change the things I can, and the Wisdom to know the difference."

That's exactly what you're doing—learning to distinguish between things you can do something about and things you can't. And, what's more important, learning how to do it right. In the future, when that Class 4 or Class 5 storm approaches, you may not be able to stop it, but you will certainly be able to batten down the hatches and prepare for it, or get to the storm cellar.

How? C.O.O.L. parents are in Control of Our Own Lives, remember. Consider the context and consequences, Observe yourself objectively, Organize your options for problem solving, Look to the future, learn from the past, and live in the present. These steps increase your overall level of awareness. You will become aware of your personal arousal level, aware of your anger level, aware of your options, aware that you are, or are not, in control of yourself. And by being prepared, you will be ready to take *positive actions* that are designed to decrease annoying, undesirable behavior and attitudes, and increase desirable behavior and attitudes in yourself and in your child.

Remember the Steps

1. Consider the context triggers and consequences of rash actions. Analyze the situation, look at your thoughts, feelings, and actions. Is it a Class 2 or a Class 5?
2. Objectively observe your breathing, body tension, and communication with self and others. Take your Personal Arousal TEMPERature (PAT) as soon as possible. You can't possibly PAT yourself too often. Do not act until you're sure your TEMPERature is in the Action Zone.
3. Organize your options for problem solving. Use C.O.O.L. breathing, deep muscle relaxation, communication (self-talk and body language) as well as imagery to get yourself prepared for problem solving. If necessary take a chill out break. Get out of there for a while.
4. Check your TEMPERature again. Use C.O.O.L. breathing, deep muscle relaxation, communication and imagery again, if necessary.
5. Replay the scene in your mind. See, hear, and feel yourself substituting more effective thoughts, feelings, and actions *before* you attempt further discussion.
6. See yourself calmly walking through the difficult situation as you chill out. Choose problem solving over screaming. Remember, you are a C.O.O.L. parent.

CHAPTER 5

Identifying Anger Triggers

The term *blind rage* refers to feelings of anger so strong that reality is blocked out. "I was in such a rage, I didn't realize what I was doing." Have you ever said that to someone? That's blind rage. It's a state of temporary insanity. In the family setting, rage of any type, blind or otherwise, terrifies and traumatizes. Blind rage can lead to serious crime. Angry adults are dangerous.

If you are an angry, volatile, hostile person, domestic violence is a real possibility. The danger of a family member getting hurt, killed, or seriously injured in your home may be greater than on the street. Your risk of being attacked by a loved one may be greater than being attacked by a stranger. When we think of physical danger, we usually think of criminals, undesirables, and hoodlums of various types, not angry family members.

The home is where the heart is, but hearts that ache sometimes seem driven to share their pain with other family members. Arbitrary anger and hostile or aggressive treatment of children is the main reason they wind up in jail or worse.

Child abuse is usually a result of anger and emotion gone awry. When we speak or think of anger gone wild, consider what has actually happened. Angry feelings have colored your sensitivity, love, and compassion. Raw rage can be invited into your life at the request of other underlying emotions as well. They are often a part of the context in which aggression takes form.

Anger is a mask that covers these feelings. Dr. Jerry Deffenbacher of Colorado State University believes that anger is the ignored emotional disturbance. He recommends that anger be categorized and systematically studied, much like depression and anxiety are today.

He is right. Angry men and women frequently lack the ability to identify, label, verbalize, and quiet their feelings. They have never been able to develop the skills necessary to make rational choices when anger is aroused. Their anger is triggered by a variety of feelings, needs, and situations. They

Become angry when they feel tense.
Become angry when they feel frightened.
Become angry when they feel worried.
Become angry when they feel jealousy or envy.
Become angry if they feel self-conscious.
Become angry if they feel ashamed.
Become angry if they feel shocked or surprised.
Become angry if they feel confused.
Become angry if they feel helpless.

For a great many people, anger is triggered by feeling sad or depressed. When alcohol or drugs are mixed with anger, rage often results. Chemically induced personality changes are often at the root of serious family violence.

Considering the context in which your anger erupts is helpful in acquainting you with a side of anger that most of us are unfamiliar with: the unconscious side. Our anger has roots that are the cause of excessive hostility. Too often we get angry without ever really knowing why our feelings are so extreme. We may think we know the reason for our anger, but if it is the product of reason, why then do we have so much difficulty moderating it?

Danielle and Todd, for example, had no real understanding of emotional diversity, let alone how emotional needs are nourished. They had to learn how to develop an exhaustive list of potential emotional needs and wants. They had to build the habit of auditing their own emotional inventory on a regular basis. By doing this they learned how to heighten their awareness of carry-over frustration. This helped them to develop the emotional resources they needed to insulate their rawer nerves.

Danielle's relationship with her husband Todd and their three children, Danny, fifteen, Melissa, nine, and Allie, eight, had been infected with the venom of the anger through which Danielle tried to grow as a child. With an alcoholic mother and a father who abandoned the family when she was eight, is it any wonder that the emotional memories of this perfect daughter continued to influence her interactions with her own children? Danielle experienced her son through an emotional prism of her childhood needs for approval and acceptance. Needs that caused her to experience a panic reaction when Danny did something wrong at school. Danielle considered herself the superstar of her family. Her kids had to be motivated to the max. If their ambition level faltered, Danielle felt like a failure. "Where is that boy's ambition and drive? Danny has so much talent I get furious at the thought of him failing." To Danielle, failure did not mean flunking. It meant failure to be the best at everything! With that definition of failure to live up to, is it any wonder Danielle stayed so angry with her son? Danny has ADD. Until she was educated about ADD, his dreamy, reticent side frustrated Danielle to the max. When she learned not to pop questions at him in rapid-fire, drill-sergeant style she discovered that less anger was triggered in her by his slowness in responding. ADD kids do much better with slow and easy, "Southern style" questions. Danielle's thoughts and emotions used to accelerate her anger. But as with the rest of us, her thoughts and emotions had a history.

It seemed as though her family moved to "Chaos Causeway" when she was born. Growing up with unpredictability, confusion, and fear, Danielle learned at a very early age to count on no one but herself, to always do what is right, to be responsible, to go the extra mile no matter what it took. Now she gets a lot of approval. And why not? This hard-charging executive certainly earns it. She feels alive at work but she is not much fun at home. Inside, she frequently feels a mix of inadequacy, confusion, guilt, and fear. This mix propels her, pushing her on to do more and more to boost her sagging self-esteem.

Her family is proud. Who wouldn't be? She is the original trophy kid. They know nothing of the pain this workaholic carries inside. Her urgency creates a deep sense of shame whenever she or someone she feels responsible for encounters even a hint of failure. She will go to almost any lengths to avoid this feeling. Supermom knows a special sort of pain when she loses control of her temper. She learned as a child always to be right. Being wrong was so scary.

Anger was and is scary. It always carried with it the threat of abandonment. She knew she could trust no one to take care of her emotional needs but herself. Is she a great person? Sure, but her inability to say no combined with her fear of failure drives her to pursue perfection relentlessly in everything she does. Everything but learning to relax. Sure, she is a great manager, the youngest woman in her company to be appointed regional sales director. She is competent, organized, and extremely conscientious. Throughout the company and community, responsibility is her middle name.

Danielle realized that her anger was a signal of something seriously wrong in her relationship with her son. She had had him partly to escape an intolerable home situation, but she is far from those days now. "Why can't I lighten up?" she asked herself. Todd loves her and has been a tremendous support system. He even passed up opportunities to advance his own career in order to move and advance hers. But she felt confused by her inability to control her anger. She was worried, embarrassed, scared, and disappointed by the absence of ambition she saw in her son. She was beginning to feel hopeless about his future. That terrified her until she began to put things into perspective.

One of the keys to resolving feelings that we don't understand is to study their history. You can do this with your feelings for your children by recreating a time line of what I call your personal invitations to anger. Every parent is issued personal invitations that keep adding up. Soon after conception mothers develop a natural protective instinct. It stimulates feelings for the children they are carrying in their wombs. These feelings can generate considerable levels of apprehension and eventually anger if Mom believes that her baby is in danger. Our earliest irritations are typically triggered by situations that tax our energy, reveal our ignorance, or document our impotence to control a dangerous situation confronting our child. Because anger is a mask, it rarely appears alone. It is almost always reactive. You might find it revealing to trace the emotional history of your angry feelings for your offspring. After birth a parent might be invited to anger by any combination of the following list of personal provocations.

Anger Triggers for Parents

Babies, Toddlers	Fatigue, Ignorance, Inconvenience, Fear
Preschoolers	Fatigue, Ignorance, Inconvenience, Fear, Embarrassment
Elementary Schoolers	Fatigue, Ignorance, Inconvenience, Fear, Embarrassment, Worry
Middle Schoolers	Fatigue, Ignorance, Inconvenience, Fear, Embarrassment, Worry, Disappointment
High Schoolers	Fatigue, Ignorance, Inconvenience, Fear, Embarrassment, Worry, Disappointment, Vulnerability, Despair
College-age	Fatigue, Ignorance, Inconvenience, Fear, Embarrassment, Worry, Disappointment, Vulnerability, Despair

Your invitations to anger may be triggered by any of these, to my way of thinking, very normal and natural feelings inspired by your offspring. Certainly this list is slanted toward high-maintenance kids. It is not exhaustive, but it should provide some clues to help you understand important aspects of the meaning underlying your anger. Danielle was driven to succeed from early childhood. By going through this exercise, she discovered that her anger was mobilized by her disappointment and impending sense of despair over her son's "low" level of ambition. But that was not all. When Danny disappointed her, she experienced more than fear for his future. She actually reexperienced the pain and humiliation that she herself had felt as a youngster who simply had to succeed. She had assumed that Danny experienced or would soon feel the pain she had learned to live with.

Her anger was motivated by a desire to protect her son's feelings. What Danielle didn't take into account was that unlike her childhood, she and Todd had created a wonderful family for their children. True, there is this anger when she feels threatened. Emotions flash her back at times to the pain of her own abusive childhood. But they are the exception. There is a great deal of predictability, love, and security in their home. When she realized she had been projecting her own pain onto Danny, Danielle's anger subsided. She began to treat him like a person. He has his own set of feelings, needs, and dreams. Danny is a very sensitive, caring teenager who enjoys helping others. He is not at all driven by the need to compete, to prove himself. As this hard-charging, executive supermom began to see her son for the person that he has become, their relationship became more genuine. She could sincerely support his decision to quit the football team in favor of spending more hours volunteering at the local Children's Hospital. As she began to understand her son's uniqueness, she began to appreciate the positive sides of the home she had created. The fact that her children do not live to escape the web of confusion, fear, and terror that she grew up in became a source of pride. For the first time she was able to step back and see her children for what they are. She remembered how much she loves Todd and began to think of what her life would have been like had she married another driven superkid instead of the compassionate, sharing, devoted man she did marry. The odds are quite good that their careers would have driven them apart instead of drawing them closer.

As we travel through life's cycle, we will receive many personal invitations to anger that we will not understand. These invitations may cause us to strike out aggressively in an unnecessary attempt to protect an invisible invalid. If you have learned what not to do from abusive parents, your child may not need so much protection. Children who have not been abused are not crippled. Often, the overprotective push isn't necessary. They have never felt the pain of your past hurts. If you did a better job of parenting than your own parents, give yourself more credit. That's the profit of your personal misery: your commitment to break that cycle of verbal and emotional abuse. The realization that your own children have not been traumatized in the way that you were should be remembered often. It will help you to accept your self as different from your child and your parents. This will give you the confidence to be more assertive with your children. Increased assertion will reduce the likelihood of aggression. When disagreements are handled directly, frustrations are less likely. Hard feelings don't have time to build up or distort your thinking.

Our drive to spare our children hurt stimulates a great variety of feelings and emotions. A richness in the variety has a great deal to do with your own family of origin, but other things also transform the energy of anger into aggressiveness and hostility. Anger is, oftentimes, a result of frustrations that have built up at work, school, or in your social life. These carryover frustrations may activate your anger triggers at home. We all have problems at work and in other areas of our lives as well. Often the angry parent is someone who has not learned how to leave work pressure at the workplace. The angry parent absorbs frustration at work, and this frustration is allowed to make anger triggers at home more sensitive. The anger trigger is then unleashed in the family setting. Take a few moments—close your eyes and imagine some of the sources of anger, frustration, and stress that you experience at work or other settings. What anger triggers are most likely to cause your next Forgettable Flare-ups at home?

(Fill in the blanks with your own experiences.)
At Work

Today at work I felt pressured when:

_____

_____

_____

In Friendships

I felt pressured and hurt when my friend:

_____

_____

_____

We all experience emotional and other psychological needs and wants. We don't always realize that they are closely related to the tension we feel, but we know tension triggers anger. If you are hungry for food, you feel tense, maybe even irritable, right? Emotional hungers work the same way. Parents forget about their emotional needs too often. Parents who neglect their emotional hunger get tense, irritable, or depressed. Some turn to destructive habits to mask emotional needs. Parents of challenging children are especially at risk. Parents of challenging children, like the nursing mother with physical hunger, need to recognize and satisfy their emotional hunger or, like the nursing mother with poor nutrition, they will provide bad milk for their children.

Review the following list of needs and wants. Find some of your emotional needs. Start thinking of ways to satisfy them. Check the words below that finish this sentence for you. Add any other words that are also important in your life.

WISH LIST: WHAT I REALLY WANT IN MY LIFE AT THIS TIME IS: _____

Vigor	Appreciation	Affection	Peace
Solitude	Centering	Privacy	Contemplation
Security	Confidence	Sharing	Devotion
Movement	Drive	Music	Esteem
Health	Knowledge	Love	Laughter
Serenity	Companionship	Poetry	Success
Responsibility	Nutrition	Integrity	Opportunity
Support	Confidence	Honesty	Energy
Imagination	Insight	Expression	Thrills
Fun	Skill	Balance	Humor
Variety	Joy	Generosity	Surrender
Relaxation	Sex	Harmony	Commitment

Happiness	Comfort	Accomplishment	Time
Communion	Beauty	Self-awareness	Control
Intimacy	Courage	Sensitivity	Serenity
Touching	Patience	Forgiveness	Humility
Structure	Romance	Money	Grace
Sleep	Trust	Faith	Awareness
Coordination	Education/Training	Receptivity	Purpose
Flexibility	Experience	Exercise	Freedom
Self-control	Tenderness	Forgiveness	Composure

Which wants have you checked? Circle the ones you can develop by yourself. Underline the ones that will require help. Help is available. Below is a list of community resources that may offer assistance in finding the help you need.

Family	Church	Friends
Mate	Community Center	Employer/Coworkers
Partner	Spiritual Advisor	Gym/Fitness Center
Teacher	Consumer Credit Counseling	Social Club
Physician	Career Counselor	Civic Club
Support Group	Psychologist/Therapist	Mental Health Assoc./CHADD

Parents may want to share their emotional needs in family meetings from time to time. It is also useful to ask older children, middle school and up, to review the emotional need chart. Ask them to complete the chart as they believe you would. Do the same for them periodically. Such a review can provide a nonthreatening way to stay in tune with every family member's emotional side.

I find the list is very helpful in my work with families. It helps people to identify what they need now. Feel free to add anything you find meaningful. As parents of very active and difficult youngsters, it is critical that you take time to nourish yourself and feed yourself emotionally. Emotional nutrition is a critical part of keeping your C.O.O.L. with your kids. We don't send children to school hungry and expect them to do a good day's work. It is just as hard for you to relate in a loving, concerned manner to your family when you are starving yourself emotionally.

Many of the emotional hungers we feel date back to deprivations that we experienced ourselves as children. Perhaps you were raised in a family where jealousy and rivalries among the children were encouraged. Perhaps there were constant comparisons between you and your brother, sister, other family members, or even neighbors' children. "Why can't you be more like Melissa?" "How come Allie always gets good grades and you always bring home such poor ones?" Statements that show obvious favor of one child over another lead to lasting hurt and deep sensitivities. These feelings are kept alive in our memory. Can you recall any sensitivities, hurt feelings, or times when you were made to feel less a person than your brother or sister at home, play, or school? Does your children's jealousy make you angry or tense? Your children's behavior may reawaken dormant emotions. These emotions may be anger triggers for you now.

For the next three days, check out your feelings. Write one or more emotions you experience for each member of your family. If you are employed, notice and record one or more feelings you experience in the presence of your boss or coworkers. If you are unemployed, a close friend or neighbor may stimulate some emotions you can log. Get in the habit of recognizing, writing, rating, and reevaluating your feelings for relevancy. Assign each emotion a comfort rating on a comfort continuum of 0, for extremely uncomfortable, to 10, for extremely comfortable. Evaluate your feelings and find out if they are silent invitations to tension or even anger. Danielle was surprised to learn that her meetings with customers and supervisors as well as Danny's teachers were almost always uncomfortable. She learned that she was uncomfortable in situations that others believed she was confident in. Great actress, huh? Many people could win an Emmy for their emotional disguises. This simple technique taught her to read her invitations to anger more carefully.

When your children's behavior makes you feel less of a mom or dad than you perceive your friends, neighbors, or relatives to be, you will experience tension. It may be conscious or unconscious, but rest assured that your Emmy-winning performances come at a high price. Learn to be tactfully true to yourself by increasing your emotional vocabulary. If a silent invitation catches you flashing back, tell yourself, "*Stop.*" Picture a happy scene. Remind yourself of something good about yourself. Some people call this self-affirmation.

"I am worthy of love and respect."

"I am a good person."

"I am making an effort to become a better parent."

Repeat these affirmations often. Remember, anger is a mask. Anger masks feelings and is often triggered by emotions from the past. Anger also masks feelings from the present. When Alice takes Eric shopping in the mall, and he runs off, she is left feeling furious, but also bewildered, frightened, and embarrassed. She vows never to subject herself to these feelings again. At the same time she is terrified. She wonders what will happen to Eric if she doesn't find him immediately.

When she does find Eric, she screams, yells, and spanks him. Alice feels guilty later. What has Eric experienced? Eric ran away, playfully perhaps, or willfully and defiantly. Eric receives a whipping, harsh words, and a message of anger. Eric was not aware of the fear Alice felt. Neither was he acquainted with the embarrassment his little invitation to anger left behind. Eric was not aware that Alice felt like a failure as a mother. All that Eric was aware of was her anger and the fear he experienced.

Anger truly is a mask. It masked how Alice felt and also how her feelings were perceived by her children. When she realized that this situation required her to gain control, she tried to anticipate in advance by remembering the importance of starting with a plan to cope. She rehearsed her plan mentally before leaving the house, then practiced the plan by going to the mall on false shopping trips. These trips had only two purposes: to teach Eric to control his behavior and to teach Alice some emotional control when shopping with Eric. Of course, she didn't tell Eric that. She simply said that they were going to the store. She reaffirmed before leaving what the consequences would be for good and bad behavior, and informed Eric that the car would be used for time-out. She also informed him that she did not believe it would be necessary. Wherever Alice goes, she makes it a point to identify a convenient corner, washroom, or coatrack she will use if it becomes necessary to time Eric out in the store.

When she parked and before she left the car, she

1. Made eye contact.
2. Reminded Eric to hold her hand and walk slowly at her side. She imagined herself feeling and behaving like some cool parents she had seen. She was certain she projected confidence in her thoughts, words, and deeds.
3. Reminded herself that the last two times they went to the store, brief verbal cues and silent prompts worked best with Eric because they really helped him *Remember* to mind.

Of course, Eric darted away in the parking lot. Alice exhaled deeply as she made every effort to grab him. Immediately and without scolding, she breathed, scanned, and released about half of the body tension that she felt. She focused on a mental picture of herself feeling calm and walking slowly. Now that she had a firm grip on his arm, she took him to the car. She also remembered that if she needed to, she would pick him up immediately and carry him. All the while, she continued to breathe, scan, and release muscle tension but say nothing. She used as little force as necessary to get him in the car. But she got him there. He sat in the car for a five-minute time-out. Alice waited until he had been quiet for ten to twenty seconds. They tried to walk through the parking lot again. Steps 1 and 2 were repeated two more times before they made it to the mall.

When you are going to practice parking lot behavior and walking in the mall, take your Walkman, or a magazine. Listen to some tapes or read during time-out. Allow half an hour at a time for this type of practice—anything more than an hour is too much. In fact, shorter, more frequent trips of fifteen to thirty minutes may work best.

Never go off and leave your child unattended in the car or at any other time-out location!

In the case of hyperactive, impulsive children, it is a matter of life and death that you adopt some kind of practice format. With compliance training, you will be able to control your youngster's behavior outside of the home. It will be most efficient if you realize that you have a right to be treated with love and respect. You have a duty to help your child learn how to do this. Never let your fear of feeling embarrassed, ashamed, or anxious stop you from being a C.O.O.L. parent. Always follow through, no matter where you are. If well-meaning busybodies attempt to interfere, thank them for their interest in your child and inform them that you are practicing a new method of discipline.

When you find yourself in a situation where time-out is impossible, take out a pen or felt-tip marker and put a mark on the hand or arm of your child. As you do so, tell him or her that consequences will result from each mark when you get home. The immediacy of the mark is as critical to success as is your following through with the consequences when you arrive home. If your child seems to really like the mark, reverse the contingency and give marks only for good behavior. By the way, this technique of reversing the uses of consequences should be followed whenever a child finds your idea of punishment fun.

Time Out and other physical discipline procedures are only useful for children up to about age ten who are not violent to you or truly harmful to themselves. Temper tantrums that involve breath holding, soiling, or vomiting are not self-destructive in my book. Unless your child has a known health problem or your physician advises you otherwise, for *medical* not psychological reasons, follow this procedure. A more detailed description of how to implement time-out can be found in Chapter 13.

Planning ahead will help you and your child deal with all sorts of transitions. If the boss is coming for dinner, or you are starting a trip, plan ahead. Clear, preferably written rules for acceptable standards of decorum, and tangible consequences, positive as well as negative, are especially useful for ADHD kids. Of course, almost all children will benefit from a little advance preparation during times of transition. Advance preparation will make you less tense and prone to anger also.

Remember, anger is a mask. Get into the habit of scanning your feelings, scanning your ego, scanning your heart. What are the triggers? What dormant memories or feelings are you being invited to reexperience? What pushes your hot button? What gets you angry and upset? Remember also what calms you down. Identify and target your emotional hot spots, the feelings that are masked by anger. You can reduce the power of anger when you discuss the feelings that it masks. Tell your loved ones what you feel. Get in the habit of talking about the shame and embarrassment you have felt. Ask others about the positive ways that they deal with these emotions. Get into the habit of defending yourself from your negative thoughts. Remind yourself as you carry your difficult child through the mall: "Yes, I do feel embarrassed and terrified when Eric disappears in the mall or pulls one of his other stunts."

Once Alice acknowledged her feelings of fear and embarrassment, she was better able to congratulate herself for her efforts to change. "Eric, like other challenging children, pulls many stunts. I know he is a difficult child and I know I am making a serious effort to teach myself how to cope more effectively."

By affirming yourself and reminding yourself of the efforts you are putting forth on your child's behalf, you will short-circuit some of the negative thinking, some of the guilt, some of the depression makers that cause your heart to ache.

CHAPTER 6

The Cycles of Change

There are ways to break the pattern of frustration, anger, and guilt for both you and your child. Ways you can control your own lives. These are proven techniques for not only surviving this experience, but actually enjoying your job as a parent! There is no doubt about the tools: They work. I've had more than twenty years experience in applying these techniques. Many professionals have done the same.

The key to it all is awareness. It is knowing how and when to apply the techniques that will enable change to occur, and it is being confident that you can do it. The way to build that confidence is to practice the techniques during times of little or no stress.

It's a bit like learning to drive a car. You didn't take your first turn behind the wheel on the busiest street at rush hour, did you? Of course not. Anyone who has ever driven a car in rush-hour traffic knows that to do so would be setting yourself up to fail. Not to mention the danger to your teacher, yourself, or anyone else who might have had the misfortune to be traveling on that road at that same time you had your first driving lesson. No, you probably had your first lesson in a more remote area, far away from traffic and other threatening distractions. Relaxation techniques should be acquired using a similar approach. Learn to relax in a quiet place amid tranquil surroundings. Once you are practiced at the art, relaxing on cue will be easy. It is at that point that you will be able to confront the enemy that is your temper.

Think of your anger as an unhealthy habit. Anyone who is ultimately successful in controlling anger may make many false starts on the journey to permanent change, for when it comes to changing behavior, persistence pays. Change is cycled through several stages, and when you understand these stages, you are better prepared to make a smooth transition. The stages of change are outlined by Dr. James Prochaska: precontemplation, contemplation, preparation, action, maintenance, and termination.

Precontemplation Stage

Precontemplation is the earliest stage. You may not even see the need for change at this point. "Why can't Barry take the garbage out without being told?" "Why do I get so angry in order to get Tracy to move off the couch and do her homework?" My patients tell me they get furious with their children for being irresponsible.

Angry, hostile precontemplators may learn about the need for change as a result of a child abuse complaint against them. Precontemplators sometimes feel that they are forced into changing. Pressure from friends, relatives, or the threat of divorce may be what gets their attention. Precontemplators may wish for change to occur, and in their hearts they realize that they are responsible for change, but for the most part they think of themselves as victims. Sometimes they don't think at all. As long as they don't think about the problem, it doesn't exist.

This ostrichlike approach to problem solving is sometimes referred to as denial, and precontemplators can be great deniers. Without accepting their part in the change process, precontemplators are left to blame others for any unhappiness they feel. Precontemplators, like Hal, sometimes blow off the need for personal change. "Sure, I've got a temper, but it works for me. Besides it's the only way I can get any work out of them. Yes, my temper is kind of short, but if I spare the rod, he'll run all over me." Precontemplators may wish for change to occur, but fail to accept their responsibility as part of the change process.

If your spouse is a precontemplator, he or she must be educated before the tools will work. If you push a precontemplator to use Action Stage tools before he or she accepts the need for change or has the confidence that the temptation to fall back into old habits can be resisted, further frustration and failure are almost certain to result. Knowledge of the stages of change themselves and evaluation of the pros and cons of change will help a precontemplator through the first three stages. The cons often outweigh the pros for many people during the precontemplation, contemplation, and preparation stages of change. The opposite is true during the last three stages.

A video about ADHD/ADD, attendance at a parenting class or

CHADD (Children and Adults with Attention Deficit Disorder) support group meeting, literature, or discussions with others may also help move a precontemplator past this obstacle. Research with habit change documents the importance of knowing when and where to start a self-change program. Psychotherapists are taught for the same reasons to time their comments and be sensitive to the patient's readiness level. We need consciousness-raising and other readiness activities when the need for change does not match the stage of change.

Contemplation Stage

The Contemplation Stage is a time when angry people are seriously thinking about how to overcome their anger. Danielle wants to change in the worst way. She accepts the fact that her anger is interfering with her relationship with her children and her spouse. She is kept awake at night thinking about her relationship with her daughter Allie. She is considering getting help, but she knows that the only way she can get her eight-year-old daughter, Allie, to listen is to yell at her. Danielle simply hasn't made the commitment yet. She has told me many times, "I know my anger is out of control. I should do more work on it. I guess there are many things I need to change about myself." Danielle is involved with the process of change. At this point, though, her involvement is limited to considering alternatives and trying to figure out just what will be involved in this thing called change. The scope of the change process is beginning to dawn on her. She is beginning to open her eyes and search for the tools of change.

At this point, she needs just enough information to help her feel challenged, but not so much that she feels overwhelmed. I recommend looking for ways to help her reduce her fear of failure and nurture her interest. She is at the approach/avoidance point in this process of personal growth. She knows where she wants to wind up, but she isn't quite sure of how to get there. Remind yourself of past successes to get beyond this stage. Recalling her success stories helped Danielle to do this.

Preparation Stage

Preparation is the stage in which personal responsibility is accepted. Steps are being taken. You are doing something to make change a reality. But temptation, cons, and fear of failure are still very evident. These issues still need to be discussed. Hank, for example, knows his temper has gotten the better of him for too long. He worries over whether or not he has what it takes to make the changes stick and he's actually started to read parenting tips that he sees in different magazines and newspapers. He is able to put some of the tips into practice; in fact, he has even begun to count to ten to cool off. Hank uses the slogan "Speak in anger, and you will make the finest speech that you will ever regret" as a thought to keep in mind when his temper heats up. Hank is trying to change; he simply lacks all the tools he needs for consistent change.

Action Stage

In the Action Stage, you actually begin to modify your patterns of behavior. You will also change your environment and associations, if necessary. Change is now a priority. You are beginning to use the tools of change on a regular basis. There is no questioning your commitment, no shirking of personal responsibility, no putting the blame off onto others. But nagging doubts persist. The temptation to smack and scream still makes it hard to be confident. Lots of support is needed now. Ask your children, spouse, or friends for it. This stage is notorious for the precarious balance between a sense of self-efficacy and the temptation to relapse. Forewarned is forearmed. There is a high risk of relapse at this point.

In this book you will find considerable emphasis on these tools. They will help you with each of the stages of change, but most specifically the Action Stage. As you are utilizing the tools of change, it is important to keep in mind that change occurs because you increase your awareness of the need for it. Change is your top priority in the Action Stage. By the time you get through this stage, you will have invested the energy necessary to learn the tools of change. As you read through this book, you will learn what the tools of change are and how to use them. At this point, you have identified your primary change targets: angry words and hostile gestures. You have even set a goal of increasing your positive and pleasant responses to stressful situations. Change will now occur on a regular basis; it will be a normal part of your everyday life since you have advanced to the Action Stage. Change feels good. Others will notice the difference in you as well.

Maintenance Stage

Maintenance is the stage where you focus on relapse prevention. Larry has made the transition. He no longer thinks about change, but acts on his thoughts. "I know what to do now. It's a liberating experience to actually be constructive instead of destructive." Larry has acquired the skills to respond to his thirteen-year-old daughter, Camille, in a positive, effective way. Larry is also beginning to see the results of his personal development. The family is happier, Camille is more positive. Larry doesn't realize it yet, but maintenance is perhaps the most critical part of the personal growth process. Maintaining positive changes is an active process. Many people think that once they've gotten to this point, change should take on a life of its own. It doesn't! The anger may be under control, but don't let your guard down. Old habits die hard.

Remember, maintenance is an active stage of the growth process. The desired changes must be consistently reinforced. You must be creative in developing behaviors that are incompatible with the old anger, loss of control, and guilt cycle. Increased personal happiness will help sustain growth. But be ever vigilant. Learning how to reinforce yourself for positive change is an important part of the Maintenance Stage. Change is a spiral process. When things are going well, you sometimes forget the tools that got you there and may slip backward. Periodic review of the C.O.O.L. Parent Quiz will help prevent this from happening. Review will also help you get back on track if you get complacent and slip off.

Termination Stage

The Termination Stage is characterized by maximum self-efficacy and minimum temptation. Don't look for this stage anytime soon. We're talking years here. But the peace of mind is well worth the work and the wait. At this point, the hard choices come easier. Because you have the skills and the confidence that come with a track record of using them successfully, the whole process of keeping your C.O.O.L.—awareness, effort, choices, emotional reactions, and behavior—feels right.

These tools will work only if you continue to use them. Think of this stage as a cross-country journey from New York to California in a car. If you continue to add fuel, oil, and water at the appropriate times, you will arrive in California within a matter of days. If instead you decide to stop the refueling process prematurely, you may never reach your destination.

When you stop using the tools, it's easy for the old ideas of entitlement to return. "I've been good long enough, it's about time these (BLANK) kids did what they are supposed to do without having to be told." Danielle's husband Todd found out the hard way. If you are not careful, before long anger will again be a regular part of your everyday life. So, too, will old feelings of depression, shame, and frustration.

When relapse occurs, and it will occur, take heart because the chances are excellent that your relapse will be temporary. Once you have identified the skills and put into practice the stages and steps of change, these temporary setbacks will become just that—temporary. Change is much easier the second time around. Whatever you do please remember this:

A FAILURE IN THE MAINTENANCE OF A CHANGE PROCESS IS NOT A FAILURE OF THE PROCESS OF CHANGE.

A failure is a temporary setback. People normally go through numerous attempts at self-change or professionally assisted change before they become long-term maintainers. Expect the relapse. Expect also to recycle upward through the stages of change. When the relapse occurs, the temptation to give up may be very strong. However, with awareness of the stage process and the tools of change, you will be better equipped to pick up the pieces and move ahead. Think of the change process as a spiral: precontemplation, contemplation, preparation, action, maintenance, and then termination. Which anger management tools will work best for you may depend on where you are in the change process when you get started.

CHAPTER 7

Systematic Goal Setting

The expression "failing to plan is like planning to fail" is particularly true when you attempt to modify your behavior.

I know my clients are serious about change when they begin to plan for it by structuring a systematic effort to tame their tempers and modify their behavior. Maybe you can begin the process of change by planning for patience as well. Structuring your plans and modifying your schedule to complete the work that will be necessary to reach your patience potential requires an enormous level of commitment. Not a thing is wrong with saying "I just don't have the energy." "These kids are supposed to show respect." "I just don't want to do all that mental training." But there is definitely something wrong in thinking you will be able to tame your temper without organizing a plan. Most of us are already overworked. Just keeping up has become such a struggle, none of us has time to waste, which is precisely why it is important for you to make a patience plan. It's the most efficient way to reach your goals. When you write down your plans and follow up on evaluating your success in completing the action steps necessary to fulfill the plans, then money, time, and energy are saved in the long run.

You will discover that writing out observable and measurable goals will enable you to put positive images to work in plans that reflect your values. By including goal setting in your temper training plan, you will get your temper under control. You will also notice an added benefit in the form of more energy and time, as planning techniques can be applied to all aspects of your life.

I know you are not training to become an expert in systematic goal setting, but I also know that parents frequently get discouraged if they don't see quick changes. Particularly those of you who tend to be perfectionistic or impatient. One of the first questions I ask my clients each session is "What in your life is working well?"

This is my way of encouraging them to focus first on the positive aspects of their situation. The reason for positive focus is simple. Too often parents see only what is going wrong. They tend to ignore what they and their children are doing right. They expect correct behavior and then ignore it. All emotions result from your interpretation or appraisal of a situation in which they occur. Anger and cynicism lead to distorted, pessimistic, or threatening appraisals. Focusing on what's wrong escalates anger and may invite defensive or retaliatory aggression. That is why it is so important to defuse habitual anger or anger that prompts hostile behavior.

Hope, optimism, and confidence, on the other hand, are the result of positive appraisals. They contribute to your sense of well-being and happiness. The belief in your ability to handle, learn from, or tolerate an unpleasant experience also contributes to your sense of personal security. Positive appraisals invite problem-solving strategies.

"What needs work" is short for "What do you need to work on today in order to become a better person tomorrow?" Identify positive goals by putting your memory to work. Recall your Success Stories, the times when you won the struggle with anger. They will provide you with a vision of what your outcome goal will look like. Your plan to achieve success will emerge from your vision of it. If you have never been successful with controlling your anger, once again pick someone you admire to be a role model for you to imitate. A mental vision of what success will look, feel, and sound like helps form the basis of your outcome goal. Next, you will develop a series of action steps to help you achieve the desired outcome.

Much of what will help you succeed involves increasing your awareness of what you do naturally that works in your favor and what you do naturally that works against your chances of success. Your personal Success Stories will help you get to know yourself better in this respect. They will build confidence in your ability to make healthy choices when angry. This is especially important if you are to get to the point of automatically making healthy choices in stressful situations. Familiarizing yourself with the psychological side of your past successes provides a friendly face to focus on. This will reduce uncertainty and suggest positive remedies when you are feeling angry. Your Success Stories offer a convenient way to access, organize, store, and reinforce positive images in your subconscious mind. This information will help you prior to and during future conflicts. Recall your finest performance when upset, aroused, and angry; a time that you felt in control of your own life even though you were frustrated to the max. Details are important. List them below. Your memory will work better if you first close your eyes, take a few deep breaths, and allow the tension to drain from your body as you exhale for a minute or two.

MY SUCCESS STORIES

My personal best problem-solving response to provocation was:

_____

Date: _____ Child: _____

Situation: _____

This success is special to me because: _____

_____

What I did right was: _____

Thoughts that helped were: _____

Helpful feelings included: _____

After the incident, what happened between my child and myself was: _____

Pause and immerse yourself in this memory for one to two minutes.

Now let your inner mind produce a word, image, or phrase that reminds you of this successful memory: _____

_____. Repeat this exercise at least once a day for the first week and never less than once a week!

Your family's values, emotional needs, social skills, and commitment level will affect your plans. The age level of the various family members must also be factored in. A little forethought will help to identify the specific action steps and constraints that must be considered to achieve your outcome goals. Outcome goals should go beyond "feeling better." Try to enumerate some of the signs you and others will be able to see that will demonstrate your subjective experience of feeling better. A sense of mission is another way of describing the outcome goals. The following shows how Larry set up his goal statement and action plans. These are the "nuts and bolts."

Larry's Mission: To rebuild my relationship with my son Derrick to the point that it was at a year-and-a-half ago. At that time, we experienced fewer than two angry exchanges per month.

Objective 1: Increase my awareness of what I think and how I feel, physically and emotionally, when my anger is aroused.

Objective 2: Learn to be more aware of context clues that precede my angry or impatient feelings.

Objective 3: Be aware of the consequences of my actions when my anger is aroused.

ACTION STEPS:

1. Complete my Success Stories to help me stay motivated and keep the big picture in focus.
2. Start an Anger Journal to help me to learn more about my Forgettable Flare-ups.
3. Keep daily notes of my progress.
4. Use Chill-Out (a form of time out for grownups. It means to simply walk away) when I am angry with Derrick until I learn more C.O.O.L. techniques.

What you choose to do when your anger is aroused can change habitual ways of handling it. Larry's Anger Journal revealed that his anger was aroused more often than he had imagined. He decided to track his flare-ups for a few days before he changed anything else. This provided him with information that would help him systematically evaluate the effectiveness of his efforts. It also provided direction to guide changes in the way he was going about these efforts. He discovered information that changed the way he thought about himself. He was able to tell what was helping and what wasn't.

Starting an Anger Journal will help to clarify the scope of the problem and decelerate aggression. A more complete description of your Forgettable Flare-ups will help you measure qualitative as well as quantitative progress. A change from hitting to slamming doors, or from slamming to shouting, shouting to chilling, or chilling to problem solving are all examples of the types of improvement that should be noted. Try the following also:

1. Note the number of times you get angry each day and how angry you get each time.
2. Keep track of your mood changes or other things that increase your vulnerability. Fatigue, PMS, pain, dehydration, or hunger are common stressors. Alcohol or drug use raises the risk of aggression to dangerously high levels.
3. Keep track of the emotions and self-talk that precede your trigger thoughts.
4. Identify the manner in which you choose to express anger and rate each incident, from 0, no anger, to 10, angriest ever. The categories below represent examples of ways people express anger.

   a. Stuff-it—defined as getting furious (0–10) and choosing to suppress your anger.
   b. Scream and shout—defined as getting angry (0–10) and choosing to yell, curse, demean others, or cut with sarcasm.
   c. Slamming it out—defined as getting angry (0–10) and choosing to bang doors or otherwise disturb property.
   d. Strikeout—defined as getting angry (0–10) and choosing to physically attack a person.
   e. Chill out—defined as getting angry (0–10) and choosing to walk away until C.O.O.L. enough to problem solve instead of fight.

5. Ask yourself what the immediate, albeit temporary, benefit of your anger was. What emotional need of yours did the flare-up fulfill? For example, a need for:

- Quiet or solitude
- Fear or anxiety reduction
- Approval or acceptance

When you have a temper tantrum and send the kids to bed, you do get quiet and solitude. If you find your lost child, anger may block, and thereby relieve, some of the emotional arousal triggered by apprehension and dread. If your flare-up demonstrated to family or friends who criticize you for being too permissive that you are not spoiling your child, your need for approval or acceptance by them may have been satisfied.

Personalize your patience plan to suit your needs. This system will benefit anyone who is truly interested in learning how to keep his or her C.O.O.L. Here are some guidelines to help you create a plan to tame your temper.

Be realistic in planning. When psychologists introduce goal setting and planning skills, they are greeted by a variety of reactions. It is not uncommon to find about one-third of the group who are very enthusiastic, another third who will use systematic planning when *they* feel it is needed, and the rest who ignore the advice altogether. Compliance is increased considerably when clear support for the system is demonstrated by the actions as well as the words of those in authority. Flexibility is also important to consider when planning to be C.O.O.L. Larry, for example, did fine with an elaborate, meticulously detailed, sequential plan that guided him through the hotspots moment by moment. His wife Kathy, on the other hand, was able to keep C.O.O.L. in the heat of battle when she carried a perspective rather than a detailed plan into stressful situations with Derrick. One thing the couple was able to agree upon was that a combination of approaches was by far the most efficient way to assimilate the concepts of systematic goal setting. Individual work, couple discussions, and total family meetings helped them to use planning principles most effectively.

When applying these principles in your own family meetings, be sure the time involved respects your children's and your spouse's, not to mention your own, attention spans and interest levels. Never spend more than twenty minutes at one time. Once the system is in place, you will discover that it becomes easier to adjust your goals, objectives, and action steps to meet your goals, based on your own as well as your family's needs. The best case scenario results when adults and children together identify and track the success of meaningful goals.

Later chapters will have lots of information to help you refine C.O.O.L. skills, but starting to plan from previous successes will get you in the right direction immediately. Plan to take actions you can do something about. Larry, for example, could require a two-hour study period, six days a week, from Derrick, to *help* get his son's grades up. He could not *require* that Derrick get good grades.

Much of what will help you succeed also involves increasing your awareness of what you do naturally that is wrong. Your Most Forgettable Flare-ups—the ones you wish you could forget but can't—are an important part of training you to problem solve when angry. They will help you profit from your mistakes. Getting to know your angry, hostile self also helps you to make thoughtful choices when these emotions are strong. This is especially important if you are in the habit of reacting, instead of reflecting, when your anger is triggered. Remembering your past screwups may be painful but systematic use of these aversive images will help you to learn to avoid repeating them. This can be used to interrupt automatic anger escalation and reduce the likelihood that you will act upon hostile impulses.

Memories of Forgettable Flare-ups can be especially useful for reducing flash anger, the no-fuse variety that gets you screaming instantly. The morning is going great until you walk by Tracy's room and see her new wardrobe scattered all over the bed and floor. Flash anger ignites instant aggression as you hurl insults and epithets in the direction of the closed bathroom door behind which Tracy is putting the finishing touches on her hair before Brad comes to walk her to the bus stop. When you periodically recall the emotional consequences of your flash aggression, you build up the strength needed to defuse it. The Three Act Play in Chapter Ten will help you get started.

Mental rehearsal using aversive images buys time to think. It also allows you an opportunity to choose problem-solving remedies when you are feeling angry. Your Most Forgettable Flare-ups offer a convenient way to access, organize, store, and use images of how you don't wish to behave. This information will help you prior to and during future times when unwanted, habitual anger is aroused. Recall your worst performance when angry. Details are important. List them below. Your memory will work better if you first close your eyes, take a few deep breaths, and allow the tension to drain from your body as you exhale.

MY MOST FORGETTABLE FLARE-UP

My personal worst problem-solving response to provocation was:

_____

Date: _____   Child: _____

This performance is especially painful to me because: _____

_____

Any of the following may contribute to aggression/violence in the family. What role did they play this time? Alcohol, Drugs, Medicine, Pain, Fatigue, Hunger/Dehydration, Other: _____

What I did wrong was: _____

Thoughts that hurt by accelerating anger were: _____

_____

Harmful feelings included: _____

After the incident, what happened between my child and me was:

_____

Pause and immerse yourself in this memory for one to two minutes. Now let your inner mind produce a word, an image, or phrase that reminds you of this painful memory: _____.

Repeat this exercise at least once a day until impulsive aggression is no longer a problem for you.

Like learning any skill, incorporating systematic goal setting requires training, practice, and application despite other needs that are competing for your attention. You will find that goal setting will help you to develop the psychological skills that are necessary to reach your long-term objectives. Here are some pointers that have been found to be very effective in helping people from all walks of life achieve their goals:

1. Set specific goals, using measurable terms and specific things you will do.
2. Set short-range as well as long-range goals.
3. Set difficult but realistic goals.
4. Emphasize performance goals (e.g., learn progressive relaxation), as opposed to outcome goals (e.g., have a better life).
5. Set goals for everyday life, not just big events.
6. Identify target dates for attaining goals.
7. Identify action steps necessary (e.g., set aside 15 minutes a day to practice progressive relaxation).
8. Evaluate goals and adjust them as necessary.
9. Record goals once they have been attained.
10. Reward yourself for achieving goals.
11. If progress is slow, check to see if you are

    a. Setting too many goals too soon.
    b. Failing to recognize individual differences.
    c. Setting goals that are too general.
    d. Failing to modify unrealistic goals.
    e. Failing to set performance goals.
    f. Underestimating the time commitment needed to see results.
    g. Failing to create a supportive atmosphere.

12. Your C.O.O.L. toolbox should also include the following:

    a. Anger Journal, including your Success Stories and your Most Forgettable Flare-ups
    b. Time line calendar
    c. Cue cards
    d. Action prompts (memory joggers that should be displayed prominently. A bit of colored paper or sticker to remind you to C.O.O.L. down will be very helpful when placed on the fridge or car mirror, for example. Action prompts work as a kind of string around your finger.)
    e. Consequences: positive/negative for *you* as well as your children.

Start small to accomplish big!

Now that you have had a chance to look over some general goal-setting principles, let's be a little more specific in applying them to yourself. Start by considering the context and consequences of your anger. What happens *before*, during, and after your Most Forgettable Flare-ups? Consider what you think, feel, and do before, during, and after each episode. This helps you to discover the physical, emotional, cognitive, and behavioral experience of your anger. Return, in your imagination, to one of your Most Forgettable Flare-ups. Take a few minutes to put your memory to work. Relax, close your eyes, and set the scene. Recall every detail of your Most Forgettable Flare-up, the one you wish you could take back.

Larry had a terrible habit of escalating the angry episodes with Derrick because he was not aware of the automatic thoughts that made his blood boil. One word led to another. In a flash he was up in Derrick's face fully prepared to wring his neck. Why? Will it help? Who knows why? Who cares? At that point, the only thing that Larry realized was that he was P.O.'d, big time! How could Derrick forget to bring home his assignment sheet from Mrs. Green? Larry felt betrayed by his son. He thought, "The ungrateful little (BLANK)! How could he do this to me?" He had taken time off from his new job to go to a teacher conference. Half a day's work was gone down the drain. He risked looking bad to his new boss. He defended Derrick to Mrs. Green. He even gave her his word that he would personally supervise the homework sessions. Now Derrick tells him he can't do homework tonight because he left the assignment sheet at school. He even has the gall to ask if he can go to Shane's house for dinner.

Larry feels his gut tighten as he realizes that Shane is the first clean-cut kid Derrick has met since moving here. "If I let him go, maybe he'll develop some positive peer pressure. Or do I enforce the rules to prove that he must be accountable? No wonder my gut is hurting." Larry is getting more furious by the second. In desperation he grabs the assignment book. Derrick "forgot" to remind Mrs. Green to make an assignment. All Larry can think about is slapping this kid silly. "Derrick is always forgetting something!"

Larry lost it. He ripped off his belt and really went after Derrick. Then he sent him to his room with no dinner, and gulped down his own food and a couple of stiff drinks. Before the news came on, he had the worst case of indigestion and a headache. Even Kathy was mad at him. He felt ashamed of himself. He was so tense he couldn't get to sleep.

Larry couldn't see it at first, but his automatic thoughts had changed his just anger into unhealthy hostility and aggression. Goal setting eventually helped him deal with the precursors to anger. He and I decided that the best way to prevent these incidents from recurring was to dissect his destructive tendencies. We used his Most Forgettable Flare-ups to help Larry learn how his automatic thoughts accelerated anger. Our plan also required a closer look at the big picture. Context analysis was the second step. Larry was aware of his global reactions. He realized what he didn't like about Derrick's behavior, as well as his own. Did he have a right to be angry? Of course he did. Was his attack on Derrick healthy for him or Derrick? No. Was it productive? Yes, in a negative way. It produced lots of guilt on Larry's part and loads of resentment and fear on Derrick's.

When you find the furies growing between yourself and a loved one, consider the context and consequences of your actions. To increase his awareness, Larry needed to learn how to detect context clues. Family conferences helped. Larry put himself in his son's shoes. We started by taking a look at the blur of the past eighteen or so months. What we discovered was that Derrick's life, as well as his dad's, had been seriously disrupted. The family had moved, which is a very stressful event for most people. One of my psychotherapy supervisors, Dr. Richard Bealka, was fond of saying, "Three moves equal a fire in terms of the devastation that can be wrought upon a family." Derrick was indeed moderately depressed since the move. Kathy and Larry had begun to fit into their new lives; even their daughter Camille had managed to make a very positive adjustment. But Derrick, starting puberty, leaving friends, and coping with ADD, still had some grieving to do. He missed his old neighborhood and friends. Through our discussions, we discovered that Derrick was very angry at both of his parents for making him leave the few friends he had and forcing him to face his insecurities in the new and scary environment. In their haste to help Derrick adjust, Larry and Kathy made the common mistake of forgetting his individuality. Camille's success fitting in made it easy for them to dismiss the significance of the social challenges Derrick experienced on a daily basis. We agreed to have Larry help Derrick through the grieving process, by acknowledging the emotional loss he had suffered and by helping Derrick fill the social void.

They planned on getting together twice a week, once on the weekend and once on a weekday to do something fun for two hours. When we pulled out the calendar and looked back at the last three or four months, not a week could be found in which they had done anything of the sort. Their relationship had been completely devoid of the fun factor. Derrick still depended on his dad for support, strokes, and good times. They were running on empty in that department. From Derrick's point of view, Dad had deserted him when he needed him most. He was angry and he demonstrated his anger passively by developing a defective memory.

It didn't take long before Derrick's memory began to improve. During their weekly outings, Larry and Derrick had a chance to take some long drives, talk, and determine what each needed to do to nourish their starving relationship. Larry began to realize how his automatic thoughts and booze were setting up the screaming sessions. This became obvious when he started writing about his Most Forgettable Flare-ups in his Anger Awareness Journal. Larry set it up in a calendar format. A journal may help you evaluate the context clues. It will help you make your Most Forgettable Flare-ups a thing of the past. Include a place for the date, time, and duration of each angry outburst, and a notation of what you were feeling and thinking just prior to and immediately after it. The significance of including all five elements lies in the need to recognize that *hostile, aggressive interchanges between people escalate because they are interactive events.* Your interactions with others when angry can be accelerated or defused because of your needs at the time as well as your behavior. My goal at this point is to help you recognize triggering thoughts, actions, emotions, and events of all types. They may come from within your self, your environment, another person, or the social context in which they occur. They act as cues that set the stage for an explosive reaction on your part. A C.O.O.L. parent must be aware of the cues that precede their Most Forgettable Flare-ups and also the consequences that follow them. What happens after the explosive episode may be just as important as what occurs before it in helping you to predict, understand, and control your anger. Larry used a lot of this information when he created his own version of the Three Act Play described in Chapter Ten.

Consider Kathy's reaction to Derrick and Camille's squabbling. Kathy set a goal of reducing her screaming in response to Derrick and Camille's aggravating exchanges in front of the TV set. To do this she decided that she would begin by monitoring her own emotional responses to these aggravating incidents. She decided that for one week she would track her reactions to Derrick and Camille. She did this by writing and rating the emotional TEMPERature of her thoughts, feelings, and behavior. She reviewed the Personal Arousal Thermometer in chapter 4. This review helped her gauge herself more accurately. She assigned each Anger episode a TEMPERature rating which ranged from "Don't touch it with a ten-foot pole!" to in the Action Zone. Her Anger Awareness Journal helped a lot. While analyzing the situations, she discovered that screaming sessions typically erupted between 6:00 and 8:00 P.M. They occurred at the dinner table and during study time. By paying attention to herself, Kathy realized she was most vulnerable after work. She was tired, dehydrated, hungry, and rushed at these times. She also realized that her fun factor in the evenings was zip. Her triggering thoughts during her ride home were along the lines of "I have nothing to look forward to but problems." Not good mood makers, those thoughts. She decided to use the long drive to listen to some soothing music. It helped her to debrief from the hassles of the day. She realized that her automatic thoughts were beginning to sound very whiny. She was beginning to think of herself as a victim, feeling used, unappreciated, and overworked by her family. The image of a pre-prince Cinderella is what came to mind.

These thoughts brought on increasing amounts of tension. She noticed soreness in her upper back and a stomach that was rarely receptive to the food she was preparing. No wonder she was on the warpath after work. After she ran off the kids with her temper tantrum, she at least had some peace and quiet. But the shame wasn't worth it. Her plan started with reprogramming her automatic thoughts. In order to combat this tendency to explode, she decided to reflect on her Success Stories. She recalled times when her patience had seemed limitless. As she wrote, she realized self-nurture was the missing element in her life. Kathy did an excellent job of interacting with people at work, but she was a bit of an introvert at heart. She recharged most effectively with quiet moments. Even the ones she had to fight for. Kathy decided she would rather switch than fight. By changing her routine, she planned for solitude instead of fighting for it.

She planned to take an aerobics class two days a week. Focusing on the movement and music in this high-energy setting can actually give your mind some time off. Kathy knew that doing something nice for herself could change the automatic thoughts and help her feel like a person instead of an object. Her next goal was to withdraw from screaming and yelling. She planned to take her TEMPERature more often. When she began to feel angry, she made a *public service announcement*. Instead of stewing, getting caught up in the automatic thoughts of being a victim, then screaming, she gave the family a "weather report" and immediately rewarded herself for labeling her feelings by taking some time out. With that, she left the area, got a bottle of ice water laced with four ounces of cranberry juice, and took a walk around the block. When the weather was inclement, she took Derrick's boom box into the bathroom along with her "mixed drink," put on her favorite Yanni CD and took a bubble bath. Thirty glorious minutes! That's all it took from reports of stormy skies to sunny ones. Kathy felt appreciated, relaxed, and empowered. Later in the book, I will give you some specific guidelines for use of time-out for your children. But all too frequently we adults forget to take time out to nurture ourselves.

When setting up your plans, remember that if you want to accomplish great things, you must start small. Begin with your Success Stories and Forgettable Flare-ups, then add an Anger Awareness Journal and provide a cue card or two to remind yourself of your plans. Write the cues that you know move you to do good things, and display them prominently. In your action prompts include reminders of what to do when you feel yourself beginning to tense up. Include consequences for yourself. Be sure to include plenty of room for forgiveness. Forgiving yourself and loved ones is an important part of C.O.O.L. living. You might even enjoy grading yourself and noting your progress on a calendar. Charting your progress and reviewing it weekly or monthly will help you to modify your plans based on results. It will also remind you to reinforce yourself for doing the right thing!

CHAPTER 8

C.O.O.L. Breathing and Deep Muscle Relaxation

People who get angry easily usually lack centering skills. Centering is a process that provides respite to any exasperated adult. It's your personal breathing room, a place you can go to turn off the hormones that are making you mad. Centering involves a decision to turn your attention inward, to focus on your own thoughts and bodily processes. It will interrupt or prevent anger acceleration and create inner peace. Centering reduces your rate of respiration, lowers your heart rate, melts muscle tension, and allows your mind to focus on the truly important aspects of the challenge at hand.

Centering is also the quickest, most accessible thing you can do to turn down undesirable invitations to anger. You can do it anytime, anyplace. It works in any situation and always feels pleasant. The ability to return to center during times of high stress is good for your physical, spiritual, and mental health.

Angry parents don't realize that the angrier they get the less efficiently they breathe. Poor-quality breathing is the kiss of death when it comes to anger management. Tension promotes shallow breathing. Shallow breathing increases tension. Increases in tension prompt distortions in thinking, body language, and voice quality that accelerate provocation. Aggressive behavior comes next. Just in case you forgot how true this is, try holding your breath for ten seconds. Do it now. Then breathe normally. Notice the tension in your body as you held your breath? Notice also the sense of relaxation when you began to breathe again? When we get angry or tense, we tend to hold our breath. This creates even more tension in our body. It also deprives our brain of oxygen, making us less likely to select our most effective options in response to the anger trigger.

Proper breathing is especially important during periods of high stress that involve children. Children are very perceptive. They read your body tension as if they have a secret kind of radar all their own. You tense up and they follow suit.

People who are quick to anger are often classic type A personalities. That's the term cardiologists Dr. Ray Roseman and Dr. Meyer Friedman and biochemist Dr. Harold Brunn coined more than three decades ago. It describes a group of attitudes and behaviors that influence a person's feelings and thoughts, and ultimately encourage the development of coronary heart disease. The doctors discovered that impatience, anger, and extreme competitiveness make men and women two to three times more prone to heart attacks than people who are low in these traits. They also described and studied a healthier, less driven personality type they called B. The so-called B types are not weaklings or underachievers. Nor are they overly lenient with their children. They are calmer and happier and possess more ability to manage their emotions, especially hostility and aggression. I guess you could say that the B types make time to stop and smell the roses. They are actually more effective in all areas of their lives. Their ability to be firm without the fury builds positive relationships. People want to please them because they are fun to be with. In essence these people are optimists who consider the context of their interactions with others, value others' feelings, and take the long-term point of view where relationships are concerned. They are able to compete without hostility. Their ability to moderate physiological arousal results in much healthier blood, business, and family chemistry.

I believe that healthy personality traits are habits that anyone can learn. All it takes is an open mind and a little practice. Emil and Alice, one couple I've counseled, made the commitment to change because the old habits were killing their hearts figuratively and literally. Their relationship was in trouble because of their reactions to their kids. Sound familiar? New ways of optimistically handling hassles not only encouraged them, but proper breathing also helped them project a more positive sense of self-worth and confidence about the future of their children.

Alice and Emil both had very definite ideas about the type of role models they wanted their children Kirk, Kelly, and Eric to experience. Kelly was only seven when Alice overheard her giving her Barbie doll a tongue lashing. That made a believer out of Alice. Kelly's play was beginning to mirror the conflict resolution styles she was living with. When your children's radar reads power plays, intimidation, and screaming sessions as the expeditious way to resolve differences, relationships suffer. Before too long they will begin practicing what they have learned from their radar reports. Adults interpret this practice as disrespectful behavior. When disrespect becomes a regular part of your children's interactions with you, their siblings, and their friends, Mom and Dad get tense and angry. If they choose healthy ways to resolve the arousal that prompts anger, their anger may have served a constructive purpose.

Anger should serve as a signal. It is supposed to energize, remind you to investigate and then consider your options, not aggress first and ask questions later. When they reflect rather than react first, Mom and Dad serve as positive role models for arousal management. Instinctively, your children want to be like you. They need your love and approval in order to feel whole. That is how society continues. Blueprints for their arousal management system are part of the package. They are created automatically as your children's radar absorbs impressions of life from those they love or depend on. From these plans will develop, for better or worse, an optimistic or pessimistic orientation toward life and love. That outlook will have a lot to do with whether or not your child becomes a discipline problem in the first place. The ability to freely and comfortably give and receive love and express affection requires a level of inner peace. Certainly not naïveté but faith in the goodwill of those who are supposed to love, support, and protect us is required for this comfort level to grow. This comfort level is a necessary part of what we call self-esteem.

People with high self-esteem have confidence that they are appreciated and cherished. Even when they make mistakes, their trust that they are worthy of love and respect sustains them. It prevents disappointment, fear, or other unpleasant emotions from becoming despair, anxiety, or shame, which too often result in a paralyzing sense of helplessness. A desperate search for "project" relationships in a doomed attempt to feel appreciated is another cost of low self-esteem. Other things being equal, people who feel appreciated are more productive in everything they do. Closely related to the need for affection, a sense of appreciation is an extremely important desire in a child or adolescent's wish to do what pleases Mom and Dad. I believe that the necessity for parents and teens to develop an adversarial relationship is grossly overrated. So often these conflicts are nothing more than fights for appreciation and respect.

That is one reason why the C.O.O.L. breathing skills are so important. The process of centering not only calms you down, but also serves as a reminder to consider the context and to ask clarifying questions when appropriate. It convinces your children that they are worthy of your love and respect even if they make mistakes that anger you. Trust and mutual respect that restores relationships or prevents discipline problems from getting out of hand in the first place is the happy result of this process. It is also vital for the development of empathy. Empathy creates a safe zone that will prevent your children from becoming addicted to anger's epinephrine rush.

Dr. Redford Williams, coauthor of *Anger Kills*, is an anger researcher who has extended the conclusions from earlier studies. He discovered that much of the type A behavior that causes heart disease results less from hostility and more from a sense of cynicism. That lack of faith in our loveability causes us to feel insecure and suspicious. It also produces overly critical and hostile behavior toward others. Needless to say relationships with loved ones are hard hit by cynicism. These traits: cynicism, a preoccupation with time, inability to smell the roses and high levels of free floating hostility make anyone not only more susceptible to heart disease but also to loneliness and heartache. Cynics are more likely to behave aggressively with those closest to them. Targets of convenience if you will. Their children will either turn out to be totally overwhelmed and broken, aggressive like their parents or passive conformists who rarely speak their true feelings and never achieve their potential, or they learn what not to do and go on to teach themselves how to give and receive the love they need.

There are many excellent exercises to promote correct breathing, and because breathing is so important it will be referred to repeatedly throughout this book. A good visual and mental image of how the breathing process works is quite important.

A picture of your diaphragm will promote a better understanding of how the whole breathing process works. It will also help you to remember to do it! As you can see from the picture, the diaphragm is a

DIAPHRAGM

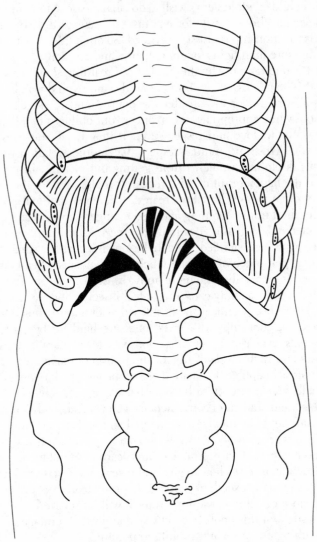

As you inhale, the diaphragm, which is attached to the lower spine, pulls down, creating a vacuum that draws breath in. It relaxes, as pictured above, as you exhale.

large, powerful muscle that crosses the body beneath the rib cage. Anchored in front at the bottom of the sternum, or breastbone, it is shaped like a mushroom or dome. It cups into the rib cage. The root of it attaches to the lower spine. When you inhale, the diaphragm is pulled down. Because the diaphragm is one of the largest muscles in your body, this action creates a vacuum in the lungs, allowing air to be drawn in. The muscle relaxes when you exhale. The diaphragm then rises back up to its resting position, pushing the air out of the lungs.

Don't forget about the diaphragm when you take a deep breath. Most of us attempt to stretch the rib cage upward and side ways as much as possible when we try to take a deep breath. Great posture for standing at attention but bad for relaxed breathing. Too inefficient. To breathe properly, the diaphragm should be extended downward at the start of a deep breath. If the rib cage and shoulders are not tense, the ribs will open automatically and the back will spread as a result of the incoming air. This way you are breathing as nature intended. Our lungs are given a chance to fill the large area created by the expanded rib cage. The diaphragm is the major air mover, of course, followed by the ribs. As you practice diaphragmatic breathing, relax your eyes. Try to feel the air going down through your body to the belt line and even beyond into your pelvis. Some imagine that it is going down even farther, perhaps all the way to your feet.

Breathing through your whole body is facilitated by imagining yourself as a flexible tube. This wonderful illustration allows you to feel deeply relaxed. Working with mental images will complement your knowledge of specific muscles. Visualizing below the belt line helps the diaphragm to descend. This enables you simply to allow the ribs to expand without force. An interesting image from *The Centered Skier* by Denise McClugg draws a comparison between breathing with the chest and breathing with the diaphragm. She likens chest or high breathing to blowing up a balloon. Belly breathing is more effortless, like the working of a bellows. To fill a balloon you must blow hard enough to make it expand. This requires energy and uses only part of the lung capacity. In contrast, the bellows open easily, allowing air to rush in; as it closes, the air is expelled effortlessly. So instead of having your lungs labor like a balloon, consider visualizing a bellows between your diaphragm and pelvis, quietly opening and closing. As the bellows works, your nostrils serve as a funnel. The ribs spread easily and automatically, first lifting and then dropping again. Allow their motion to become the result of breathing, not the cause. As the bellows expands, in flows the oxygen; as it contracts, out goes the carbon dioxide. You will experience an extra measure of tranquility by attending to the sensations throughout your body as you practice C.O.O.L. breathing.

The Science of Breath by Yogi Ramacharaka was published in 1904. This little volume devotes ninety pages to the benefits of breathing. One need not be an oriental philosopher to experience the benefit of the following natural tranquilizer, called the Yogi cleansing breathe. It is said to cleanse the lungs and stimulate the cells, and also to tone the respiratory organs and be generally conducive to healthy conditioning.

1. Inhale a complete breath.
2. Retain the air a few seconds.
3. Pucker up the lips, as if to whistle. Vigorously exhale a little air through the lips.
4. Stop for a moment, continue to retain most of the air.
5. Repeat this process of vigorously expelling air through the lips, stopping for a moment then continuing, until all the air has been exhaled.

This simple exercise has long been valued by the Yogis for its ability to refresh one who is feeling tired and "used up." Most of the parents I see are quite familiar with the tired and used up part. I thought you might find the Yogi cleansing breath useful when you feel that way, too. Speaking of feeling tired, this style of breathing is also very popular with the Olympic and professional boxers I had the pleasure of working with for over fourteen years at the Roy Jones Boxing Gym in Pensacola, Florida. They believed that it helped them conserve energy, remain calm, and be more effective during training and competition. Hopefully this alternative can help you to make the right choices when you feel fighting mad.

C.O.O.L. breathing took Alice and Emil giant steps along their journey to reasoned, effective responses to Kelly, Kirk, and Eric. Those kids were the worst when it came to forgetting instructions. Talk about feeling fighting mad, Emil's TEMPERature gauge used to stay locked on boil-over during the nightly homework hassle. Centered breathing helped make these Class 4 emotional storms a positive, if not a pleasant, experience. Some people find that inhaling for a count of four followed by holding their breath four seconds before exhaling for another four counts works great, but Emil felt that he achieved more success by extending the cycles to eight counts each. Hence the name: The Rule of Eight.

The Rule of Eight is a mnemonic device that is easy for parents to remember and has proven very beneficial to my psychotherapy clients. With this simple tool, they rarely forget to breathe properly when they need to. Centered breathing is one skill that will make your children take you seriously. You'll learn how to C.O.O.L. down and stay C.O.O.L. when you discipline or instruct them.

Children see that you mean business by your C.O.O.L. demeanor, and begin paying attention when you speak. You will project yourself as confident. The pleasant emotions you feel when you know that you are doing the right thing will reinforce your behavior; making you more likely to be consistent in your approach. Make sure you have eye contact with your child as you instruct him or her; your child will take you seriously when you do. These skills—centered breathing, deep muscle relaxation, communication, and visualization—are key components of the C.O.O.L. technique. They make it possible for you to achieve your goals.

As you inhale for a count of eight, hold it for an eight count, then exhale for a count of eight, it is helpful to pay attention to your body signals during the inhaling, holding, and exhaling process. Study the muscle tension as you first experience, then release, it. What happens if you only count to six, or if you're feeling so comfortable you decide to count to ten? Not to worry. If it works for you to vary the count, do it. The Rule of Eight will work for most people as a starting place. Finding your own C.O.O.L. Zone may be the most important part of the program because, as you learn to find your own C.O.O.L. Zone, you are also learning about the limits of your body-mind relationship. By all means, be creative in your self-discovery. If it's comfortable for you and not dangerous to yourself or anyone else, and most of all if it's effective, do it! A reassuring sense of Control of Our Own Lives is the natural result when we are more effective, calm, and composed with our children. An added bonus is that this will hold true when applying principles of reward and especially punishment to your child. Remember children often get off on your anger. Anger then becomes a reward, not a punishment. Centering activities will also prevent you from focusing on unrealistic thoughts that accelerate anger. The following exercise will show you how to tell if you are breathing properly.

It is easier to learn to inhale comfortably if you start by learning how to exhale comfortably. That way your lungs will have a lot more room to expand. Start like this: Get comfortable in your seat. Sit with your feet flat on the floor. Breathe normally. Now place your right hand on your stomach and your left hand on your chest. Exhale, then inhale as deeply as you can. Notice as you inhale which hand moved first: the hand on your stomach or the one on your chest.

Now repeat. This time make the hand on your stomach move first. See yourself making a potbelly as you inhale, pushing your stomach down and out. This way you'll have your diaphragm working in your favor. You will fill your lungs with air from the bottom up.

Now inhale, pushing down and out, filling the lower lungs first and then allowing the air to flow up, filling your entire lungs with air. Allow, don't force, your chest to expand as you draw more air in. Remember the bellows below. Hold your breath for an eight count. Then, exhale for an eight count. Breathe like that three or four more times until you get comfortable with belly breathing.

If you forget how to do C.O.O.L. breathing in a tense situation, no problem. Just concentrate on exhaling. Let it out slowly and the odds are good that you'll inhale properly and receive the same relaxing effect. Practice this method of breathing from time to time throughout the day and you'll soon discover that you're doing it automatically, without effort. In fact, most people who develop the deep breathing technique soon find themselves doing it a lot. It is healthful and energy-producing.

We've seen that you can't be tense and calm simultaneously. That is why deep muscle relaxation is also a vital factor in your ability to remain calm and effective in difficult situations. Deep muscle relaxation is an efficient response to tension from any source. It reduces the rigidity that our bodies experience when we get tense. It is an effective tool to help us remain C.O.O.L. when we're dealing with difficult kids, relatives, or any stress-filled situation. Muscle scanning, stretching, and relaxing is particularly helpful for buying time to consider your alternatives. It should become one of your automatic choices when you receive a surprise invitation to anger. It helps you to pause, and by doing so, you will interrupt the escalation cycle that often causes angry emotions to result in hostile choices that lead to ugly incidents.

Numerous biological changes take place when we get alarmed, approximately fifteen hundred by some estimates. These changes prepare us for action. When that action gets hostile, we contaminate our bodies as well as those of our families. Heart disease, even cancer, have been linked to hostility. As a family psychologist, I can assure you that hostility is a heartbreaker for your children, relatives, friends, and coworkers as well.

Today's medical literature and popular magazines are filled with news about the relationship between mind and body. It is in vogue these days to emphasize biochemical causes of behavior. Biochemical causes of depression, attention deficit disorder, and almost any form of aberrant behavior frequently make the nightly news. It is true that biochemistry is a factor in these conditions. It is also true that many of our body's chemical changes have to do with hormones triggered by tense muscles that have accepted too many invitations to anger. Remember those changes in the muscles in your jaw, the back of your neck, and across the front of your head? Once you learn to deal with these changes, you are well on your way to being more effective as a parent. Some ways of dealing with biochemical changes cause us more stress and pain. Some people smoke, some eat excessively, others abuse alcohol or take drugs. Some throw temper tantrums, and—well, you get the idea. For now, let's talk about the C.O.O.L. parent's way of dealing with the physical arousal that accompanies anger: awareness of the context, breathing, release of body tension, and communication. The use of deep muscle relaxation will help you get rid of the tension.

To develop this skill, set aside thirty minutes each day for a week or so. Select a comfortable chair. Many people use a straight-backed chair for this purpose. Position yourself so that you can stretch out your arms and legs. Remember to use what you've already learned about C.O.O.L. breathing. Inhale with a relaxed, controlled motion. Many people discover that it is easier to learn relaxation exercises if they have a tape to guide them. Progressive muscle relaxation

and some of the breathing and visualization exercises lend themselves to being taped by you. With taped exercises you are free to
focus completely on the physiological and emotional sensations you
experience. I remember my first experiences with taped relaxation
exercises were much easier to follow because I wasn't straining to remember which step came next or distracting myself by wondering if
I was doing the steps correctly.

If you do make a tape, use it only until you can perform the exercises confidently. You may also want to use the tape to prepare for, or
relax after, a particularly stressful situation. My patients typically wean
themselves as I did by learning to scan and release muscle tension
throughout their day. They practice whenever or wherever they get a
few moments. Stress expert John Mason suggests that you either make
the tape yourself or ask a friend to make one for you. If you make your
own tape, you may need to allow some time to get over being self-
conscious about hearing your own voice. This is easily accomplished
by listening prior to your first scheduled practice session.

Speak slowly. The taped voice should be about one-quarter your
normal rate of talking. Use a calm, monotone voice. Frequent pauses
for ten to twenty seconds will allow you to relax even more deeply.
At the end of the tape, "wake yourself up" by counting from three to
one. Raise your voice and quicken your pace to communicate alert-
ness as you count.

You are going to learn how to systematically create first tension
and then opposing muscle relaxation in specific groups of muscles
from your head to your toes. You will also be instructed to acquire
the habit of scanning your entire body for muscle tension, and then
to release any tension that you discover. The idea is to tense slowly
so that you can notice small increases in tension. You will release
quickly. Allow time, ten to twenty seconds, as tension is released.
This will help you notice small increases in relaxation as well.

We'll work with each area of the body separately. But once you
have become more familiar with the technique, you'll be able to
combine exercises, thus working on more than one area at a time.
You are encouraged to customize the technique and work on those
areas where your tension bothers you most often. This should be a
pleasant experience. If you experience pain, *stop immediately*! Consult your physician to find out why. You are either overdoing it or

some physical problem needs to be considered. You may want to use the following description to make your own tape.

Remember, tense in SLOW MOTION and release quickly.

1. Tense slowly, and release quickly.
2. Compare and contrast the sensations of tension and the relaxation response.
3. Be aware of the just noticeable differences as tension and relaxation levels change. Close your eyes. Take a deep breath and hold it for a count of eight. Then exhale, long and slow, for a count of eight.

1. Fists and Forearms

Tense your fists and forearms slowly. Be fully aware of how your hands and arms feel as you increase the tension. Pay attention to your fingers, knuckles, palms, backs of hands, and wrists. Attend also to the top and underside of the forearms. Hold that tension for a count of eight. Remember, tense only your fists and forearms.

Relax every other part of your body. Keep your jaw, forehead, and shoulders relaxed. Focus on feeling the tension in your fists and forearms. Hold tension for a count of eight. Now release. Notice the feelings of relaxation flowing into your hands and forearms within ten to twenty seconds after you let go.

Allow yourself to feel deeper and deeper levels of relaxation as you go through this process.

Again, now tighten your fists and feel the tension in your wrists, fingers, and forearms. Hold it for an eight count. Let it build. Then relax. Learn to appreciate the difference between tension and relaxation.

2. Biceps

Next, we'll move to the biceps and make a muscle, like Popeye. Keep your fists relaxed. Keep your shoulders relaxed and calm. And, most of all, notice whether your jaw, face, and back are relaxed. Don't allow bicep tension to seep over into these other areas.

Tense up. Make a muscle. Slowly feel the biceps tensing. Hold for a count of eight, relax for a count of eight. Notice the relaxation response.

Now repeat. Tense the biceps, notice the feeling of tension. Hold. Relax the biceps. Study the feeling of relaxation.

3. Triceps

Now we'll move to the triceps, the muscles in the backs of your arms. Raise your arms to shoulder level. Push straight out from your shoulders to the left and right. Push away from your body with the palms of your hands. Notice the tension in your arms under the biceps, in the large muscle that runs down the backs of your upper arms. And push . . .

Hold that tension.

Relax. Let the tension go. Notice the difference between the two feelings.

Repeat. Tense the triceps. Hold and study the feeling. Release, and feel the difference.

As you relax deeper, you may notice feelings of warmth, heaviness, or perhaps a tingling sensation in your arms. As you progress, you'll probably notice similar sensations in other parts of your body. That's great!

4. Forehead and Scalp

Now let's move to the forehead and scalp. Close your eyelids gently. Raise your eyebrows. This will cause wrinkling in the scalp and forehead. Notice what this feels like, because this is the area where headaches often occur.

Hold and study for an eight count. Now release it and let it go.

Try it again. With your eyes relaxed, your jaw relaxed, your neck relaxed . . . close the eyelids, lift the eyebrows, tense the forehead and scalp. Feel that tension. Study it. Then release and study the difference in feeling.

5. Eyes

Next, we'll move to the eyes themselves. This is easy. Just close your eyes tightly. Feel the tension building for a count of eight or ten. Study the tension—then let it go.

Repeat the process, being careful to keep the other parts of your body relaxed.

6. Jaw and Mouth

Next, move to the jaw and mouth. The jaw is an area of primary concern. A tight jaw frequently goes along with stress-related headaches, and it is a very easy one to notice and keep track of.

Bite down slowly but very firmly in the back of your mouth. Pull your lips back as you do. Feel the tension radiating out from your jaw. Study that tension and then release it.

Do it again, and attend to the changes between the feelings of tension and the feelings of relaxation.

7. Throat

Let's move to the throat. Press your tongue against the roof of your mouth. Feel the tension in your throat. Try to keep your jaw relaxed. Release the tongue pressure, relax. Now repeat.

You will experience yourself going deeper and deeper into a relaxed state as you become more familiar with the sensations. Enjoy this pleasant experience. That is exactly what you want to do. Allow the muscle tension to melt away.

8. Neck

Let's move now to the neck. You can tense the neck by putting your chin on your chest and then gradually rotating your head in a circular motion until your chin is back on your chest. Slowly let your chin rise and notice the relaxed feeling, compare it to the tension that was there before.

Now let's go in the other direction. First, chin on chest, rotate your head around, all the way back, finishing up with your chin on your chest.

Release, relax. Notice the difference.

9. Shoulders, Upper Back

Now attend to your shoulders and upper back. Continue relaxing your jaw. Let go of any tension in your hands or your eyes. If you notice tension in any of these places, just release it. Release the tension and prepare to "be calm" in any situation. Experience yourself as calm, controlled, and competent. Now shrug your shoulders; raise them up and see if you can touch your ears with the tops of your shoulders. Begin slowly, methodically. Notice the feelings. Now roll your shoulders back, and then forward. Slowly, methodically. Look for the slightest changes in the tension levels. Repeat.

NOTE: It may be a little difficult at first to isolate contracting and relaxing muscle groups. Stick with it; you will improve greatly after just three or four practice sessions. I want you to be able to identify surprise sources of tension; because as you're opening that report card or opening the door to Jamal's room, I want you to scan your body and release any tension you discover as well as exhale.

Now let your shoulders hang loose. After a while it will help you simply to imagine rolling your shoulders forward and back, without actually doing it. Repeat the shoulder exercises once more, and now let's move on to the chest.

10. Chest

Expand your chest fully as you take your deep breath. Fill up your lungs but this time flex the chest. Feel the tension building. Hold it. Study it. Let it go.

Study the relaxation.

Now repeat. Expand the chest. Hold and study tension. Release and study relaxation.

11. Stomach

Now we'll move to the stomach. (Often there's a tight ball in the stomach that causes indigestion, diarrhea, or constipation.) Focusing inward, slowly suck in your stomach. Study this feeling and release tension in other parts of your body as you do this. Study the feeling as you try to pull your belly button all the way back until it "touches" your backbone.

Hold it, study the feelings. Let it go, study the feelings. Repeat.

Now we'll do just the opposite, pushing your belly button outward until you make a potbelly. Feel the tension as you do so. Hold it. Now let it go. Notice the relaxation.

Repeat that process.

And now I want you to tense the muscles of your stomach without sucking them in or pushing them out. Just flex all those muscles, and notice that feeling.

Again, see if you can tense the abdomen without tightening your jaw or your shoulders. Then let it go. Notice how it feels as you relax. Repeat.

12. Lower Back

Move to the area right behind your stomach, the small of your back.

Tilt your pelvis forward just enough to feel the tension in the small of your back. Hold that. Then let it go and study.

Repeat the exercise.

Tense and study—release and study.

13. Buttocks and Upper Legs

Lift yourself up on your seat ever so slightly by tightening your buttocks. (Don't push off with your back or feet.) As you flex the buttocks, allow the shoulders to remain loose. Remain as relaxed as possible everywhere else and feel the tension in the buttocks and upper legs.

Release and study.

Repeat.

Flex and study. Release and study.

14. Lower Legs

Now the lower legs. Extend your legs out in front of you. Lift your feet and lock your knees. Feel the tension. Hold it for a count of eight, just enough to become really aware of the tension as it builds.

Let it go. Notice the feeling of relaxing muscles.

Repeat.

Extend, flex, and study.

Release and study.

15. Lower Legs and Feet

Next, the lower legs and feet. Allow your heels to rest on the floor and curl your toes up toward the ceiling so that you feel tension in the shins, the front part of the lower leg. It may take a while for you to feel this tension. Study the feeling. Release, and study that feeling.

Repeat.

Tense and study.

Relax and study.

Allow your toes to curl down. Pull them toward the floor so that you feel the tension in your calves as well as your toes. (Ideally, shoulders as well as all other parts of your body should remain relaxed.) Study the tension in your calves and feet. Release, and feel the difference.

Repeat. Study the contrasting feelings of tension and relaxation.

16. Scan Your Entire Body

From head to toe, releasing any tension that you experience. Now with your eyes closed, take a deep breath. Hold it a little longer than you've been holding it (a count of ten to twelve will do nicely, more or less if you like) and then let it go. Breathe naturally, deeply, and slowly. Scan your body for any source of tension that may have crept back in. Scan and release tension in the face, neck, arms, shoulders, back, chest, abdomen, buttocks, legs, and feet. Release this tension. Just let go of it, and feel the calming overall relaxation. Now in your mind's eye imagine that you are bending your right arm. *Do not physically move it.* Only imagine that it moved. Notice the sensation of muscle tension and movement you experience without moving at all.

This is the type of practice that you should advance to. When you can reliably produce muscle tension and relaxation using the stretching exercises, I recommend that you rehearse the movements in *your mind only* until you can release body tension without flexing first.

In time, you'll be able to feel the tension and relaxation by use of your imagination alone. The experience will become real by simply creating it in your mind. The good news is that you will become even more relaxed. As you mentally picture your muscles relaxing, you will let go of tension and create the changes in your body that will regulate your level of physical arousal.

You will become better as you continue to practice. It's best if you can practice the deep muscle relaxation twice a day for one week, more if you prefer. Rate your level of body tension before and after each training session. I suggest that you use a simple ten-point scale for this purpose. For the first week, follow the steps pretty much as I have outlined them. Then, as you get more comfortable with the technique and are capable of doing the isolated tensing and relaxing steps easily, you can begin to start grouping areas together.

Your eyes and forehead, for example, can easily be worked on together. And you can work on your upper arms and hands all to-gether, your chest and stomach and so on.

The key is to be able to identify specific points of tension or specific parts of the body where tension gathers. It is different for every one of us. By relaxing those areas that are tension traps for you, you will become more skillful at decelerating anger. By the way, these techniques will help your relationship with your spouse, your other children, or any part of your life that provokes tension.

CHAPTER 9

Practicing Imagery

Seeing with your eyes closed, often called visualizing, is a valuable tool for keeping your C.O.O.L. Visualization is also known as imagery. With imagery you see and experience yourself in a way that helps you to relax, feel more confident, and achieve specific goals. Imagery is also helpful when you want to develop a specific skill. When your images are positive, they energize and inspire creativity. The opposite effect may result from negative images. Unfortunately, most adults and many youngsters have been programmed with too many negative and not enough positive images. Gary learned how to change that for himself and for his children by learning more about how imagery influenced his life.

For some time, he had struggled with emotionally laden images. They provoked excessive anger towards his stepson. Gary had a hard time feeling relaxed and comfortable with Quentin because the boy reminded Gary so much of Quentin's father, Ed. Quentin's father never did accept his divorce from Brenda. Ed constantly undermined Gary and Brenda. Blending two families can be difficult when adults cooperate, but Ed didn't know the meaning of the word. When they came at all, his child support checks were late or "just a little short this month." That was aggravating enough, but it seemed that Ed was using his relationship with Quentin to get back at Brenda for divorcing him. He would build Quentin up to expect a weekend visit to dad's house. Full of anticipation, the boy would be all packed and ready to go ahead of time. Come 5:30, no Ed. 6:30, no Ed. By 7:30, Josh was crying because Quentin had "accidentally" hurt him while they were wrestling on the floor. His apology rang about as true as Ed's did on Sunday. The whole incident was brushed off when Ed called about 4:00 that afternoon. Seems that Ed had been called out of town unexpectedly. "Sorry, Quent, we'll do it next week for sure."

Although he was only nine years old, Quentin had begun to forget to do his chores. He also forgot to return change when sent to the store for a loaf of bread. He was also forgetting how to be gentle with his younger brother. At four years old, Josh idolizes his big brother Quentin. Gary knew he needed to do something to develop more patience with Quentin. What made him furious was that just when he and Quentin were starting to build some bridges, Quentin would hear from, miss a visit with, or get his heart broken in some other way by his father. After that, he would clam up or get mean and sneaky. Gary could be understanding to a point, but it was difficult. The kid looked and acted so much like his father it was scary. Gary could feel himself withdrawing from Quentin. At such times, he could almost see Ed when he looked into Quentin's dark brown eyes. Gary just couldn't give him the benefit of the doubt, Brenda said. Gary was really starting to get overprotective when it came to Josh. She believed that Josh was beginning to play up the victim role to get Quentin in trouble. The pay-off for Josh was the attention he received when he was rescued. Unfortunately, he was too young to realize that this was starting to encourage even more hostile behavior from his brother.

As Gary and Brenda began to analyze the context in which their anger was being played out, they realized that they were allowing Ed to disrupt their family and seriously undermine Quentin's emotional development. Their anger was self-defeating. They both got so angry with Ed's excuses that they let him off the hook. They weren't assertive. Their failure to confront Ed's irresponsibility nullified their complaints. The best they could think of was to try to ignore it. They got too angry when dealing with Ed to do much else. Unfortunately, because of Quentin, they had no choice. The problem with Ed was not going to go away. They could have worked on just trying to ignore the situation and wait until Quentin was able to confront his father directly. Their values, however, dictated some action on their part until that occurred.

Brenda and Gary decided to develop a plan to restructure their relationship with Ed. As she thought about what her goals might include, Brenda realized that she had a lot of negative expectations of Ed. Gary shared this negativism. Together, their expectations of past behavior were dooming any hope of improving things for the future. Because the mere mention of his name created annoyance or low-level anger, discussions about Ed usually increased the tension to the moderate range. Ed's excuses, threats, and denial of responsibility triggered anger in Gary, and guilt in Brenda.

They both took some time to analyze the few Success Stories they had had from their dealings with Ed. It became obvious that their only chance for success was to calmly and consistently repeat one simple message: Quentin was very disappointed and hurt by his father's unreliable behavior.

It wasn't much, but it was a beginning. If they were going to reach their goal of increasing calm communication with Ed, they would have to practice. Action steps to achieve this goal included becoming more aware of low, medium, and high levels of anger arousal. They knew they needed to PAT themselves (check their Personal Arousal TEMPERature) a lot more often if they were to have a chance of interacting with Ed in a constructive way. They rehearsed the script which stated simply, "Quentin gets very sad and angry when you fail to keep your appointments to pick him up. I'm sure you want what is best for him. I would like for you to pick him up on time or call when you are going to be late." Brenda and Gary took turns role-playing a scenario that eventually involved calling and communicating this message to Ed. Using their Forgettable Flare-ups, they reconstructed scenes they were likely to face again when they actually made the call.

Actions steps for carrying it out included observing and releasing body tension, belly breathing, positive self-talk and using a positive image that communicated strength and power. For Brenda, focusing on the image of a tigress helped her to experience feelings of power and confidence. For Gary, images of sailing served this purpose. Feeling the wind and experiencing the sound of the breeze in the sails freed him from inhibitions that sapped his energy and cleared the cobwebs from his thinking.

Action steps included visualizing the call to Ed, experiencing all that would entail. Rehearsals included breathing rhythmically, feeling tense, and releasing some of the tension. Practicing relaxing, positive inner dialogue such as, "I can handle this" and "I will remain calm," helped prepare them for the call. They rehearsed continuing to take deep breaths as the phone rang. They also visualized a successful, calm, problem solving discussion in which they would stick to the point and not get blown off course.

Brenda tried, she really did. Whenever she got to the point of actually seeing Ed in her images, she could feel her body stiffen, palms perspire and breathing become shallow. Then the image disappeared. She simply could not get to the point of actually speaking calmly to him. She got stuck initially because this image generated too much negative emotion. If this ever happens to you, put some distance between you and your image. Intense images tend to be an up-close and personal in-your-face type of thing. They can be vivid, noisy, and colorful. Reduce the intensity and make the situation less threatening by viewing the scary scene from a distance, in black and white or through a fuzzy lens. When you are comfortable with the fuzzy image, you can make it a little sharper. DON'T MOVE TOO FAST! When a new image causes you to feel vulnerable, anxious, or angry, return to a less threatening one.

Adding a humorous spin to threatening images will also make them easier to handle. One of my clients, who was on the other side of a broken heart, recently had to interact with her old flame. She was having all sorts of emotional turmoil. Flashbacks were causing her to feel sad, tense, and powerless. Carla imagined Dave dressed in a "Porky Pig" costume as she mentally rehearsed her meeting with him. It worked so well that she had to restrain herself from laughing when the meeting finally did take place. Brenda tried the same approach very successfully when she spoke with Ed on the phone.

When the call was actually made, Ed was initially quite defensive. At first, he attempted to laugh it off and trivialize the problem. As he realized she was serious, he tried to put the blame on Brenda. Telling her if she hadn't divorced him, they wouldn't be in this situation. For her part, Brenda ignored that and simply repeated her concern and request. Whenever Ed would attempt to get back to giving his lame explanations, Brenda avoided the temptation to call him a liar. She simply continued to scan, relax, give a very quick reply, such as "Oh, I'm sorry to hear that," and then, like a broken record, repeat her concern for Quentin and her request. Though it seemed like hours, the entire conversation lasted only two or three minutes.

Gary and Brenda knew they had only begun, but they were very proud of themselves. The mental rehearsal had actually helped. They were able to profit from using images to feel themselves beginning to tense up, reminding themselves to release the tension and to stick to the point without escalating the conflict or retreating. Later that evening, they treated themselves to a movie.

The term *imagery rehearsal* usually refers to imagining yourself successfully doing something, whether it's dealing with your children, speaking with an ex-spouse, or getting a promotion at work. By mastering imagery you will begin to experience mental images as though you are looking at the real event. At this skill level, when you are using imagery to improve your problem solving in provocative situations, you will even be able to see, hear, and anticipate the approach of the real event. Your physical, mental, and emotional reactions to the situation or person involved will be very realistic. You will *not* see yourself reacting. It won't seem as if you are watching home movies. It will seem as though you are actually speaking face-to-face. All highly successful people use imagery. Imagery will help you control emotional arousal, learn new skills, or perfect existing skills. It is valuable for learning to execute abilities under pressure, reduce butterflies, or change attitudes. Imagery facilitates learning how to regroup after a mishap and how to soothe hurt feelings.

All behavior is a result of images that are stored in your memory. Without movement memory, we would not be able to get out of bed or tie our shoes. We couldn't remember how to move without our mental images. Olfactory memories keep your lover's scent alive. Without images of taste, we would have no favorite food because we could not remember what our favorite food tastes like from one meal to the next. Without images of sound or touch, we could not remember what a hug or kiss feels like from one day to the next. Mental images create the blueprints for practically all human activity.

Anyone who can daydream can visualize. Some people see images better than others, but anyone who wants to use imagery can learn how. Many people see only fleeting images at first. As you become more skillful, you will experience more of the image.

If you would like to improve your ability to use imagery, follow this simple plan. Only ten minutes' practice a day will produce significant improvement in your imagery skills.

The Six-Day Imagery Play

Day 1

A quiet place is nice, but not necessary, for your first imagery lessons. Take a few minutes to begin your lesson before getting out of bed or going to sleep. Begin with static visual images. Mental pictures of very familiar objects is a natural place to start. Imagine them as completely as possible. We know that the more specific and detailed your image is, the more benefit you will derive from practicing imagery.

You might look at the lamp in your room, then look away and try to imagine the lamp. Use only your mind; keep your eyes closed. Rate your image for clarity, from 0, for a blank screen, to 10, for virtual reality.

Close your eyes and picture a favorite article of clothing or a piece of fruit for thirty seconds. Evaluate the quality of the image by asking yourself for details. Did you see a new or wrinkled garment? Press for details. When you can form a realistic mental picture, repeat this procedure with five familiar objects or pictures. Take about two minutes per unit from image to critique.

Evaluate each image for thirty seconds, describe the image for one minute, then go on to the next image and description. A sample list might include: an apple, a purse, a car, a photo, or a favorite garment. Whenever you experience difficulty forming the mental picture requested, take a peek, then look away. Something of your own choosing, something that you are very familiar with, such as a favorite shirt or your mother's face, may be easier to begin with. Practice forming mental pictures as you go about the day, both at and away from home.

Day 2

Let's experiment with sensory images. What is your favorite food? First recall the taste of your favorite food. Close your eyes for approximately thirty to sixty seconds to reactivate the taste memory. Use several minutes if you so desire. Now open your eyes and ask yourself to experience the food in your mouth. Is it cold, warm, or hot? Is it fluid or solid? Moist or dry? Chewy or crumbly? Evaluate the quality of your tastebud memory. Follow the same time sequence used with simple image recall.

Next, ask yourself to reexperience movement memory by reliving some physical activity that is meaningful to you. It may be as simple as brushing your hair or as involved as a round of golf. Recall it with as much detail as you can. In golf, for example, feel the stance, the grip, the swing, and the follow-through.

Day 3

Recreate one of your Success Stories or Most Forgettable Flare-ups. The exhilaration of your Success Story or the pain of your Forgettable Flare-up is stimulated by emotional images. Emotional images are stored in your subconscious, the same as all other images. Emotional images are useful for helping parents prepare for unpleasant situations. Happy outcome or celebration imagery will help lift sagging spirits. Emotional images can help you keep your C.O.O.L. They will help you to control and reproduce your optimum level of emotional arousal and energy when you need it most.

Start by visualizing your Success Story performance. Make the images as vivid as possible, include all senses—sight, sound, smell, touch—especially at the emotional level. Notice and rate (0 to 10) your emotional arousal level prior to and during your most successful encounters with your anger. I call these your peak performances. Consider a rating of 0 as the lowest, 10 as highest level of arousal. Close your eyes, and recreate the peak performance image. Pay close attention now to your emotional arousal level when at your best. Allow your inner mind to produce an image that reminds you of these feelings, just as you did with your Success Story earlier. Open your eyes. Do this with several peak performances, and notice the energy level that seems to be most consistent with you at your best. Continue this exercise anytime you have a few minutes to spare.

Be conscious of thoughts, actions, and activities that help you either to mellow out or to raise your emotional arousal level when needed. Develop a sense of your ideal level of negotiation arousal. This will help you stay focused during tense discussions. With a clearer notion of how your emotions affect your ability to work through your anger in tense situations, you will experience more consistent success in keeping your C.O.O.L.

Day 4

Your thoughts or self-talk are very important. They may cause tightening of your muscles. Your thoughts may encourage fatigue, cause you to press too hard, or otherwise cause you to lose your focus of concentration. This can be very unnerving in tense discussions. Self-talk that results in either giving up or trying too hard clearly removes you from any opportunities to succeed. You can learn to be more aware of your negative self-talk and to appreciate the value of substituting positive self-talk in critical situations. Imagery is useful for facilitating the acquisition of this skill.

Visualize a set of circumstances in which anger causes you to lose focus. Recall your thoughts and feelings at that time. Ask yourself, "Are my thoughts helping me to refocus and make healthy choices in this situation?" See yourself substituting positive self-talk that helps you to refocus and keep your C.O.O.L.

Day 5

Your feelings and emotions, masked by anger, are influential in raising your TEMPERature. They cause tense muscles and encourage you to press too hard, or otherwise lose your focus of concentration. As with your thoughts, this can be very unnerving in situations involving anger. Negative emotions rob the energy necessary for making and sticking by healthy choices. You can learn to be more aware of the impact of negative emotions and appreciate the value of substituting positive emotions in situations that involve anger. Imagery is useful for developing this skill.

Visualize an angry situation in which you lost focus. Recall your masked emotions and feelings in that situation. Ask yourself, "Are my feelings or emotions helping me refocus?" See yourself experiencing more positive feelings that might be helpful in refocusing concentration.

Day 6

Visualize a set of circumstances in which healthy choices of thoughts, feelings, and behavior allowed you an opportunity to resolve a difficult situation that you would have previously mishandled. Allow yourself to experience all the positive effects that resulted from this behavior. Consider this a victory celebration. Victory celebration imagery is useful for motivation and should be a part of your overall imagery program.

Practice both types of imagery. Alternate celebration images with images of proper execution of C.O.O.L. tools. Be creative. Remember that there is no right or wrong way to use imagery. Variety, experimentation, and the development of your personal touch will help you discover what works best for you at different times in your life.

You can use imagery training to program your blueprints for living. Know what types of images you learn quickest and you will be on the way to knowing how to program your mind and body for success. Some of us learn quicker by concentrating on things that are associated with sights. I have a very talented surgeon friend who attributes his success in medicine to an uncanny ability to see a surgical procedure only once and commit the procedure to memory.

Many great skiers say they can see the hill in their minds' eye before they even begin down the slope. The skiers' mental vision is internal, not an image of watching themselves ski down the slope. Rather, they see only the slope with their inner vision. Inner vision is just like seeing the slope, or anything else, through your own eyes. The slope is seen just as it appears to the skier when he or she is physically skiing down the slope.

Muscle images are the physical equivalents of the other sensory images that make you tick. Muscle images actually cause physical changes in our muscles, nerves, body fluids, hormones, and other body functions. When was the last time you blushed? When was the last time you flushed with anger? Muscle and physical images are very important in learning to keep your C.O.O.L.

Just imagine tensing and bending your arm at the elbow to make a muscle. No cheating—don't move your arm. Just imagine that you are moving your arm. You will feel the muscle memory tensing the muscles in your arm almost as if you actually did flex your biceps. Muscle tension is the reason you get so tired just sitting and worrying.

Sound complex? It's not. The important thing about the discussion of images is to realize that God gave us many wonderful ways to influence ourselves and others. If one way isn't working too well, we can always try another. All our memories, thoughts, feelings, moves, sights, sounds, and smells can help us to help ourselves and loved ones.

Relaxation imagery benefits parents and children. Using imagery will help you to experience hope for better things to come. By projecting into the future, you will get the benefit of positive results and happier times before they get here. The two types of imagery most commonly used are outcome and process imagery. With outcome imagery, you see the results of your labors of love. In process imagery, you use images as tools to help you refine your skill in performing the steps needed to reach the goal of keeping your C.O.O.L.

Parents of challenging children often get discouraged. I believe that imagery can help you deal with that discouragement in a constructive way. If it works for professional athletes, Olympians, and captains of industry, why shouldn't it work for parents?

Consider an example. You have a splitting headache. Eric is teasing his sister, Kelly. The noise is excruciating. You respond, "Eric! Why do you always have to pick on Kelly when I have a splitting headache? You are driving me crazy! Why can't you be more like your brother, Kirk? Kirk never—" On and on you go.

Later, you realize your anger has contributed another layer to your own and to Eric's negative self-esteem. You feel guilty because once again you let go with a verbal barrage. But what could you have done differently?

Consider this scene again. Imagine yourself handling this situation differently. You have a splitting headache. You hear Kelly screaming. But this time you choose to behave like the C.O.O.L. parent you are:

1. You take your TEMPERature and block trigger thoughts.
2. You breathe—breathing is important. Remember to belly breathe as you scan and release body tension.
3. You tell yourself, "This is a tense situation, but I know what to do."
4. You use the STOP sign technique to further disrupt negative thoughts. Say to yourself, "STOP." See a bright red STOP sign.
5. Using imagery, you visit your special place for a few seconds or minutes. Your visit will interrupt the sequence of anger development and will help you C.O.O.L. it down.
6. You pause to imagine yourself calmly separating the children.
7. You continue belly breathing, releasing muscle tension and encouraging positive communication with yourself as well as your children.

Finish the scene by reinforcing yourself for handling the situation so well. Perhaps your favorite aunt, who has been observing your interaction with your children, comes over and gives you a big hug and tells you what a good mother you turned out to be.

You can also use imagery in other areas of life, for example, by allowing a favorite place to come alive somewhere within your consciousness. Experience it. It's a place where you always feel calm, safe, relaxed, confident, and happy. Be there now! Experience yourself in your special place. Feel your senses come alive there. See, hear, touch, smell, taste, and feel whatever you discover in your special place. You are there in mind, body, spirit, and emotion. You are feeling joy, peace, and happiness. They are alive and well within you. Your confidence grows. This sense of well-being that you experience now is carried with you like a warm glow. Repeat this thought: As it is in my mind so will it be in my life. This is *your* special place. You will return to it in times of need.

Your special place can serve you in several ways. Certainly your special place is at your disposal anytime, anywhere, to help you unwind and to C.O.O.L. your temper. Your special place also gives you an opportunity to enrich your ability to experience imagery. Use imagery creatively. Use novelty as you feel comfortable with it. Most of all, find a special place that helps you achieve the goals of inner peace, calmness, confidence, relaxation, and tranquillity.

Your special place can be an important part of a tool called thought stopping. Many parents get caught up in a cycle of aggravation they would like to break. They want to break it because they know it is harmful for their children and it also leaves them feeling guilty. Thought stopping can serve as your ounce of prevention. Thought stopping can help you catch anger early in the sequence and react constructively. Anger researchers tell us that anger is a sequence of thoughts, feelings, then actions. If you catch yourself early in the process, you will be able to recognize that your thoughts are actually accelerating the angry feelings and leading you to hostile actions. You will redirect angry energy into more positive outlets.

CHAPTER 10

Three Methods of Anger Management

The Three Act Play

Becoming a C.O.O.L. parent is a bit like producing a play. *The Three Act Play: My Invitations to Anger* is a metaphor. Think of it as your personal anger brake, as well as a technique that will teach you to reprogram your automatic responses to anger triggers. The purpose of the technique is to show you how to interrupt your automatic anger response or flash anger. Flash anger is one of the most difficult types of anger to control. It seems as if your TEMPERature goes from a healthy 98 to a deadly 108 in a heartbeat. Using vivid recollection of the unpleasant consequences of your impulsive release of anger will help you stop them. It will allow time to learn positive methods of influencing your children.

The three act format is designed to use your feelings about past failures to program you for success in the future. Every play needs a setting, story line, script and characters. Your Situation Barometer will provide the setting, and your Most Forgettable Flare-ups and Success Stories should provide you with plenty of story lines. Start by selecting a scenario from your Situation Barometer. Choose one that you are confident you can handle. As your skills improve, move on to more challenging roles.

First you must set the stage, learn your part by rehearsing C.O.O.L. skills mentally, then go out and perform.

To do this you should, as they say in show business, get in character. Actors are encouraged to live the part they will be playing to help them create realism, and it makes for a much more convincing performance. The C.O.O.L. parent system asks that you develop a vision of how you will appear in your new role as a C.O.O.L. parent. This is how you put your imagery lessons to work for you. A process of mentally rehearsing living as the new you will help you do this. Identifying positive role models, recalling you at your best and practicing positive self-talk are all a part of it. Core centering skills such as belly breathing, progressive muscle relaxation, communication and imagery should be rehearsed. The guidelines found in this book will give you many options for developing and refining these skills. Practice until you are quite comfortable with them. Once you are comfortable with the core skills, you will be ready to choose the setting, develop the plot, set the stage and learn your lines. Dress rehearsals will come last, of course. Opening night is your opportunity to show your self and family what you have learned.

Depending on your family schedule, opening night may be at six in the morning. As you walk by the door to your teenager's room, for example, you are reminded of the limits of your influence. Mess is too kind a word to describe the site. Boiling may be too cool a term to define your TEMPERature. What a way to start the day! Or at 3:30 in the afternoon when the school bus comes rumbling down the road, discharging its cargo of little people, you feel the knots in your stomach tighten. Your Situation Barometer is the list of incidents that make you angry. Use it to identify 5 invitations to anger that you want to turn down on opening night. Arrange your situations in order of their ability to produce anger. These trigger situations should include at least one or two of your Most Forgettable Flare-ups.

The last props that you will need to get arranged prior to your dress rehearsals are your Success Stories. These are your memories of you at your best with detailed accounts of the times you have handled your anger admirably. This might have occurred in a situation involving someone other than your child. Include any situations in which you were able to get a grip and behave appropriately when you were really struggling with anger. If your Success Stories are in short supply, or if you have never had a successful experience in this regard, recall a positive role model. Select someone you admire, much like Danielle did, or choose someone you have never met, such as someone from TV. Selecting a positive role model is important for all of us. Getting in the habit of noticing positive people will

help you stay C.O.O.L. permanently. If it is difficult for you to identify someone to imitate, discuss what you are trying to do with a
friend or therapist. They may be able to assist you by helping to open
your mind to a wider range of appropriate behaviors. Additional information on healthy options will make it easier for you to choose
wisely when your anger trigger gets squeezed.

Remember to start small if you plan to accomplish big things. Try to
focus on a specific situation that makes you angry often. That way you
will have more opportunities to practice self-restraint. From your list of
triggers, select a situation that you believe you will be able to master
with practice. Regular brief rehearsals of two to ten minutes are more
effective than occasional longer ones, and you will find the Three Act
Play can be a very rapid method of changing your hostility habits. You
may not require too many rehearsals before you begin to see progress.

Before you begin rehearsal, set the stage for Act I. This occurs as
you read or think about a time your temper took you too far. In Act II,
vivid memories of the emotional pain caused by your Most Forgettable Flare-ups is created by immersing yourself in the aversive images
of your past screwups. Then in Act III, you are to switch to your Success Stories, or those detailed recollections of successful scenes to
elicit constructive thoughts and healthy emotions, so you will relive
pleasant memories of processing your anger by using the C.O.O.L.
tools and rules. Your ability to organize options for productive problem solving when angry will be strengthened as soon as you recall
those successful efforts to make healthy choices in the past. Your Success Stories will enable you to prevent painful scenes in the future by
granting you access to memories that, all too often, get forgotten in the
heat of passion. Replay scenes you hope to avoid often. Practice may
not make you perfect, but it will take you a whole lot further than waiting until your child runs away from home, or you give up in despair.
The rehearsal schedule for the three act play goes like this:

ACT I: You will imagine the trigger scene you are hoping to
change. Start by relaxing yourself for a minute or so. Sitting in a comfortable place is nice but not totally necessary. If you get stuck in a traffic jam, you can rehearse your part there as well. Simply change the
story line to help you master highway hostility. Imagine the trigger
scene for 30 seconds to a minute. Recall your Forgettable Flare-up in
considerable detail. Concentrate on the anger you felt at the time.

Feel as much of it as possible. Try to make it real. Rate your anger level 0–10. Ten is the most you ever felt, 0 is none at all. When you are able to feel your anger, convincingly, hang on to it for one to two minutes. At this point, you should be able to recreate the scene, reexperience the emotion and rate it for intensity. When you can do this, it is time to switch scenes. Bring the curtain down on the angry memory.

ACT II: While you change the set, immerse yourself in your memories of the negative consequences of your Forgettable Flare-ups. Larry recalled how horrible he felt as he saw the bruises he had put on his son. He immersed himself in the emotional consequences of his Forgettable Flare-up in Act II. Get in touch with the embarrassment, the shame, the fear and hopelessness that you have felt when you realized that no matter how you attempted to handle your emotions, they never changed. Hold on to those feelings for a minute or two. Feel as much of the pain as you can tolerate. When you can do this, it is time to drop the curtain again. (Note: If this procedure is too painful, obtain the assistance of a mental health professional.)

ACT III: Switch scenes from misery to mastery. This is the time to use your Success Stories, but first set the stage. For example, in the case of the messy room, see yourself waking up in a good mood, walking past the open door to the dirty room, and beginning to get angry. Now exchange that hot thought for a cool reminder to STOP! See the bright red STOP sign in your mind. As you do, move away from the door. Communicate constructively with self-talk, body, and words. Return to your bed and sit down on it as you belly breathe. Scan and release your body tension as you sit there. Applaud yourself for steering away from your fury rather than directly into the "eye of the storm." See yourself recalling a painful reminder of your weakness where anger is concerned. See also your child's vulnerability. Recall your constructive self-talk, "he needs friendly firmness," "I'll talk to him about his plan for his room tonight when we have time to do it calmly." Congratulate yourself by recalling a happy memory. A pleasant recollection of your son meeting some new friends on a vacation, perhaps. Recall as much of the happiness in that situation as you can. Be sure to include your feelings as well as your thoughts.

Don't forget the credits. Tell your child what you are attempting to accomplish. Let friends and other family members in on your plan as well. *Ask them to congratulate you for taking this important step in trying to control your anger.* They may also be able to assist by gently reminding you to stay in character if you forget your lines.

Dress rehearsals will prepare you for opening night. How many re-hearsals are required for each item on your hierarchy? It will depend on your willingness to practice and also on how successful you are at effecting changes in aggravating situations. Reliving memories of your Forgettable Flare-ups and recalling memories of Success Stories will get you ready for opening night. The supporting cast is an important part of any production. Consider including family and friends in yours. Tell your child and others what you are trying to do. You may even ask them to give you feedback. Develop a signal they can give that lets you know that you appear angry to them. Obviously, this cue should be given in a polite, respectful manner and accepted by you as such.

Be sure to reward yourself for working with this program. There is no specific amount of time that you must spend rehearsing. Continue working with each item until you are able to switch scenes comfortably. The more C.O.O.L. skills you can bring into mastering imagery, the more options you will have for productive problem solving.

The Three Act Play can be a very emotional experience. The Time Machine, however, can be a less intense way to tap into emotions that will help you put your indignation in perspective.

The Time Machine

Anger often results when our attempts to cope with stress are misguided by pessimistic trigger thoughts. At times, our needs to be a good parent cause us to get overly critical. Too many shoulds and oughts can make it very difficult to live up to expectations of what a good child or parent is supposed to think, feel or do in a given situation. Particularly when the proscriptions are based on solid logic that is supported by a foundation of false premises. When you are trying to tame your temper you need good information on age-appropriate behavior and emotional needs of the object of your irritation. This can be disillusioning to parents who were all prepared to enjoy this experience, especially if they are the proud parents of the high-maintenance child.

When your child requires extra care and attention you would do yourself and your child a big favor by learning as much as you can about the circumstances surrounding her needs for extra attention. This will support your positive thinking and perhaps allow you to be less vulnerable to negative thoughts triggered by insensitive comments and inappropriate expectations or demands of friends, family, teachers and neighbors. Pessimistic people are more prone to experience unproductive, overly emotional responses to threats or danger. That is the last thing you need. Precious little is closer to a parent's heart than their child, it is natural to want the best for them. Sometimes, we simply forget that our children aren't finished yet. A ride in the Time Machine can help you to lighten up and be more optimistic. It is also a wonderful vehicle for teaching lessons in humility. Humility can do wonders to help you keep a C.O.O.L. perspective by reminding you of youthful indiscretions that taught you valuable lessons in life.

It works like this. If you know you have been rather hot-headed lately, you probably have filled out at least one Forgettable Flare-up sheet. Whenever this happens, take a trip back to a point in time when you were the same age as your child is now. Think back to a situation that is similar to the one that just got your goat. Select a specific incident when you got in trouble because of a mistake, misunderstanding, or disobedient act. Start your trip by taking some belly breaths and releasing muscle tension. Allow your mind to focus on the house you grew up in or some other reference point for that period of your life. When you can see your room, look around in it. Notice the color of the walls. Look first at the window, then out of the window. Open your closet or dresser drawer and find your favorite garment, memento, or plaything. Perhaps there may even be some pictures or notes lying about. If so, examine them in detail. Once you are reacquainted with your old surroundings, switch scenes and go to the incident you are trying to recall. If you are able to go directly to it, by all means do so at once. Use the detailed inspection to reactivate your memory as needed.

Write down what happened to you that day: _____

_____

_____

What had been your plan: _____

_____

_____

Who was with you: _____

_____

_____

What went wrong: _____

_____

Who caught you in the act: _____

How you felt when you realized you were in trouble: _____

_____

_____

Anything ironic or humorous about the event: _____

_____

Take a ride in the time machine when your TEMPERature starts getting too hot too often.

Me, Myself, and I

The best actors and actresses need direction. Me, Myself, and I combines many of the elements you have been reading about and practicing. It is especially helpful for coaching yourself through provocative situations. It emphasizes communication with self and is very useful when you are interacting with the person or circumstance that triggers your anger. This "stress inoculation" technique was developed by Dr. Ray Novaco and has been helping people for over 20 years. It is a sort of checklist of helpful self-statements to use at various points in an interaction that is provocative. I have modified and shortened it, but the structure remains.

Preparing for a provocation while you are waiting for a stressful situation to develop is a typical way people use stress inoculation training. It is very common to have a lot of negative thoughts when you anticipate trouble. Unfortunately, negative thoughts waste energy and detract from problem solving. Angry people frequently focus on feeling helpless, victimized, or entitled to better or more equitable treatment. If their beliefs lead to constructive activity, great. Unfortunately, they usually serve to increase arousal to the point that is counterproductive in one-on-one or small group situations. This leads to blaming, accusing, or other destructive methods of discharging a lot of unpleasant emotion. Try to use self-talk that emphasizes mastery instead of misery in this situation. Here is our Three Act Play, expanded into five acts.

ACT I—PREPARATION FOR PROVOCATION

I know this could be very upsetting, but I have been practicing. I know how to deal with it.
I'll try not to take this situation too seriously.
Time for some cool, belly breathing, scanning, and releasing.
No need to fight, I'm here to problem solve.
If he gets unreasonable, I change my goal for this meeting to practicing C.O.O.L. skills.

ACT II—THIS IS IT. UP-CLOSE AND PERSONAL. YOU ARE ACTUALLY FACE TO FACE.

The purple hair almost got to me.
Stay calm. Continue belly breathing.
Look at a point on the wall just above his head.
We are apples and oranges. Neither is better, just different.
This is not a contest for me.
I'll search for the positive.
It's a shame she must behave like this.

Might as well relax, breathe, and release tension.
He must be very unhappy to behave like this.

ACT III—I'M COPING WITH AROUSAL.

What is working well and what needs work?
I feel my jaw and shoulders tensing. Time to let go.
My goal for this meeting is to avoid getting hooked.
He must feel very threatened.
I may just have to disappoint him, but I'm not getting angry over this.
My anger is a signal. A cue to remind me to belly breathe.

ACT IV—REMINISCING WHEN CONFLICT IS UNRESOLVED.

What worked well, what needs more work before our next meeting?
I am improving at this.
If I could have done better, I would have done better.
Next time, I'll picture him dressed up in a "Tinkerbell" costume.

ACT V—WHEN CONFLICT IS RESOLVED
OR COPING WAS SUCCESSFUL.

I met my goal of keeping my anger in the low range all but one time.
I'm proud of myself.
Compared to last meeting, I improved 50 percent.

You can change the script to meet your needs. By going through this process, you will have a greater sense of personal control.

CHAPTER 11

All Work and No Play: The Recipe for Burnout

Finding the fun factor in your life is an important part of keeping your C.O.O.L. Burnout breaks up many happy homes. It leaves us feeling used, unhappy, and irritable. Burnout is the result of too much seriousness and too little laughter. Worrying about kids, work, and sick or aging relatives can drain your energy. When money or other problems seem so important, fun is neglected. Often fun is left for later. Unfortunately, for too many people, later never comes and the fun factor is left out of their lives for far too long. Ironically, when your world seems at its worst, self-nurture is the one thing you can control. You always have the power to do something nice for yourself, regardless of your other problems.

Self-nurture is more than important for happy family life. It's essential for good mental and physical health. A happy mood increases personal effectiveness. Pumping up your mood strengthens your ability to accomplish all types of things. Researchers have found that if they teach people how to pump up their moods, they set higher goals, persist at them longer, and have high levels of confidence that they will achieve them. The implications of this research in the area called self-efficacy are obvious for parents who are struggling to believe that they can eventually control their anger as they look to a lifetime of living with a challenging child. This is one of the reasons why it is so important for you to roll your credits and recall your Success Stories. Parents who have a strong sense of self-efficacy try harder and persist longer when faced with a difficult task.

Learning to laugh at yourself and your situations is an important part of keeping perspective. I have noticed that worry warts and other frustrated people do a great job of avoiding fun. This can create an atmosphere that makes "madness" more likely. When our needs for fun are ignored, we start to feel neglected. Chronic neglect of our self can cause us to become more protective of the free time we do have; worse yet, it fosters the notion of entitlement that increases the likelihood of angry retort. "Hey, the least I should get is some peace and quiet when I get home" becomes a battle cry, as we get grouchy when we feel neglected. Neglecting the fun factor is not to be taken lightly. It is important in every aspect of life. How many times have you heard professional athletes say, "I'll keep playing until it's just not fun anymore."

Increasing the fun factor has always been of primary importance in my work. In fact, rating the fun factor in their lives is one of the first things my clients are asked to do, as part of my initial evaluation of their needs. Lack of fun leads to burnout. Burnout sometimes turns to depression. People who are depressed lose the capacity to experience pleasure. Some lose the ability to have fun at all. Many people who are depressed are also very irritable and angry. So the vicious cycle regenerates itself and we take out our feelings on our children.

While there are many ways to help depressed, irritable, or angry people cope with this lack of interest in pleasurable activities, I find that the direct approach of encouraging them to begin doing things that were once pleasurable can produce positive results in a relatively short time. My own research in relating the fun factor to personal stress, depression, and anxiety supports this finding. Researchers investigating happiness are beginning to discover that happiness and unhappiness are not opposite ends on the same emotional continuum, but separate feelings that can exist simultaneously in each of us. While it is true that a predisposition toward sadness may be inherited, happiness seems to be more situationally controlled.

In a study of more than one hundred pairs of twins, many were found to be much more similar in levels of unhappiness than in levels of happiness. Identical twins have also been found to be more similar than fraternal twins in their levels of unhappiness, but this is less evident in levels of happiness. These results suggest that while tendencies toward sadness or unhappiness may run in families, happiness may be more subject to personal control and the influences of your environment. Other studies completed at the University of Minnesota compared personalities of identical twins who had been raised together with those who had been raised apart. The twins who were raised together were more similar with respect to their levels of happiness than the siblings who had been raised apart, but there were no major differences between the groups with respect to unhappiness. Science writer Diane Swanbrow believes that these findings may offer some useful clues to people wishing to live happier lives. The moral seems to be that if you focus on things that make you happy and do things that make you happy, you will be a happier person. In my own research on stress, anxiety, and depression, I find that the fun factor is related on several levels to personality adjustment. When we get stressed out with our children or other problems, we tend to stop doing things that were once fun. This increases negative thoughts and the stress that goes with them. Once again, it's a vicious circle. Improving the fun factor in your relationship with your child will have a great bearing on the amount of anger you experience.

This occurs for several reasons. We are naturally drawn to people who are more upbeat and positive. Children are naturally fun-loving and will almost always work harder for teachers who are creative and who incorporate fun activities in their work. They will work harder to please just about anyone whom they perceive as a fun person. Fun people tend to smile more, to notice the good in people, and to encourage positive personality traits. For these reasons, it is extremely important that fun be a big part of your anger-management program.

Be sure that you leave plenty of room in your schedule for fun. Most people make the mistake of leaving the fun factor to vacation times or special events. Unfortunately, family vacations, particularly with difficult children, can often be more trying than fun. Fun with your children will be more productive if you select activities carefully. Remember that children who tend to be impulsive frequently have a short attention span for fun activities. There are some exceptions. Many children seem to be able to spend endless amounts of time plugged into video games, but for the most part, activities that adults consider fun, such as sports, hobbies, and games, are built around sets of rules that require patience, organization, and paying attention.

Make a special effort, when organizing fun activities for you or your children, to remember their limitations. Remember also the limitations of your patience. If you decide to take your child on a fishing trip for fun, think hard and long before you plunk down any money to go out on a boat or get out on a pier. Many children will have a lot more fun and you will, too, if you plan on going some-place close to home, where you can spend an hour or less, and where you can enjoy the outing rather than teach your child something like fishing. When you are going to take a hyperactive child fishing, don't plan on fishing yourself. Simply be there to help, monitor, and enjoy. If you do decide to fish yourself, don't get very serious about it. Leave your type A personality on the beach!

When Emil takes Eric fishing, he uses the same rationale and follows the same procedures Alice uses when she takes him shopping. He makes certain that he spells out the consequences for good and bad behavior in advance and sticks to them. Normally, Eric is much better behaved with his father. We don't know why for certain, but ADHD boys generally are much more compliant to their father's requests than their mother's. In his best-seller *Men Are from Mars, Women Are from Venus*, Dr. John Gray argues persuasively that there are significant differences in the male and female communication styles. These differences are well documented by other researchers. Dr. Gray believes that, in general, men speak less and act more. They give fewer warnings and quicker consequences. To the extent that this is true, it would help to explain the reasons that boys in general, and high-maintenance ones like Eric in particular, are more inclined to do what a consistent, caring male tells them to do.

Adults also need fun activities away from the children. This is one of the primary needs of couples who are struggling with anger. If you are short on money, select low-budget activities that you enjoy. Go to the dollar movie instead of the first run, walk on the beach, or in the woods, or take a trip to a museum. Going bowling can be a lot of fun, particularly if you don't take it too seriously. Planning your vacation or a trip can be almost as much fun as going. Many times, people who are angry or impatient spend so much time doing things that they miss the enjoyment of anticipating.

Make finding competent child care a priority and at least once a week go out on some kind of date where no family business is discussed. Single parents should do likewise.

If you are having difficulty scheduling fun in your life, return to the basics. Recall activities that were once fun for you and commit yourself to getting reinvolved with them. Remember, when it comes to fun, half a loaf is better than none. For many years I enjoyed off-shore sailboat racing. This is a tremendous adventure and a great deal of fun. But the amount of time and energy needed to get the boat and crew race ready was enormous. I don't know about you, but time has not been too readily available for me during the great economic recovery. Massive increases in red tape due to managed care, and a maturing family that now includes a new extended family and a darling granddaughter, have filled some of my fun slots with work or responsibilities. A decision to try my hand at writing and research at mid-life has, temporarily, gobbled up time once available for sailboat racing. So instead of campaigning my own boat, I have opted to become a crew member on other people's boats. This enables me to have all the fun of sailing with a minimum of hassle and none of the expense.

Trying new activities can be fun if you keep your expectations of success reasonable. If you tend to be perfectionistic or are easily embarrassed, use your C.O.O.L. imagery skills to imagine getting through the awkward, early stages of learning some activity that you want to become better at. Dancing, for example, can be a great deal of fun. Some people, mostly men, are self-conscious and avoid doing it altogether. But taking lessons can be a very successful way of learning to loosen up, take yourself less seriously, and have some fun in the bargain.

If you have been struggling with a bout of the blues or burnout, and activities that once were fun no longer appeal to you, force yourself to get started doing them anyway. I encourage depressed people to increase the fun factor in their lives whether they like it or not. Those who forge ahead with activities that once were fun may not enjoy them initially. But after several weeks of participating, they will enjoy themselves almost as much as they did before. Often just making the decision to do something fun for yourself is empowering. If this is difficult, remember the importance of measuring results. We measure to reinforce ourselves for making progress. If you are in a phase of burnout, your thinking may tend to be all or none. Be very careful to rate your experiences of fun accurately in the beginning. When you are grouchy and irritable, anything you do may take a lot of effort. You may be tempted to quit because it seems so hard. Quitting at this stage is a big mistake. Remember that planning to increase the fun factor is like planning anything else. You must start small to achieve big. With realistic goals, fun will eventually find its way back into your life.

Most communities have fairs, craft shows, and a whole range of free things that can be done to have fun. Fun can be as sedentary as collecting stamps or stones, or as active as skydiving. It doesn't really matter what the fun activity is. What matters is that you get out and do it. Many people derive a great deal of enjoyment from reading jokes, cartoons, and humor pieces in newspapers. Learning to tell jokes can also help you be more sociable and comfortable with new people that you meet. Try to see the funny side of various predicaments that you and your children experience; irony is often a part of the problems you face.

CHAPTER 12

Taming the Time Monster

Many people are so caught up in the rat race they can't see their way out of life's maze. Our perceptions become our reality, and determine how we will react. But too often our reactions are negative. Some angry people feel overwhelmed because they focus on personal productivity and fail to recognize the significance of building relationships, especially relationships with their children.

Time also affects our relationship with our children. If you find yourself thinking "If that kid had any ambition, he would have a decent job by now. It makes me furious to have to keep forking out money to support him," your perception of time running out triggers a whole series of negative images that are destroying your relationship with your child. Even though your anger is triggered by love and concern for your child, it is misdirected emotion.

Anger rooted in our love for our children can lead us to panic when time appears to be running out on our dreams for their future. In *The Road Less Traveled*, M. Scott Peck, M.D., beautifully states the value of commitment. "Commitment is the foundation, the bedrock of any genuinely loving relationship. Deep commitment does not guarantee the success of the relationship, but it does help more than any other factor to assure it." Committed parents do experience the pain of disillusionment and fear for their children's future. These feelings continue until they believe that their children are well on their way to independence. The harsh economic reality that the current generation of American children will be the first to have a lower standard of living than that of their parents serves only to further frustrate and aggravate the empathic parent.

With more than one-third of America's children being raised in one-parent households, time can tug at your temper in other ways as well. Attempting to balance the roles of provider, protector, and teacher without the support of a spouse causes nerves to stay on edge a lot more than we would like. While anger is not a necessary result of frustration and worry, we do know that it commonly occurs in situations where stress associated with time pressure is greatest.

Speaking from personal experience, it is not difficult at all to notice how my own tendency to over-include activities and projects can create angry exchanges with family members, frustrated clients, or disappointed friends. When you feel the pressures of time, you need to analyze your values.

In his national best-seller, *Seven Habits of Highly Effective People,* Steven Covey raises two questions. Question one: What one thing could you do (that you aren't doing now) on a regular basis that would make a tremendous difference in your personal life? Question two: What one thing in your business or professional life would bring similar results? Covey believes that their are four unique human endowments: imagination, conscience, independent will, and self-awareness. These, he believes, form the foundation of personal habits that define our basic character. *Habit* he defines as an internalized pattern of principled behavior.

Lindsay, for example, found herself in a situation not unlike that of other single mothers and fathers today. Fiercely independent, she despised her inability to better herself financially. She also had a very strong commitment to motherhood. It triggered feelings of guilt when she had to leave her children in day care. With travel and overtime, this often totaled more than fifty hours a week. It was obvious that something had to give. In answering the first of Covey's questions, she felt that spending more time with her children on a regular basis would make a tremendous difference in her personal life. As far as question two was concerned, she believed that getting more education would enable her to get a better job. She simply had to find a way to use her time more effectively. She decided to begin the process of prioritizing.

By clarifying in her own mind what was really important, she was able to get her personal effectiveness program off to a good start. She remembered what she had learned about value-based decision making at a seminar some time back. Now was as good a time as any to dust off those notes and see if they might help. Value-based decision making includes ethics in a behavioral value system made up of values, attitudes, and beliefs.

Values are the basis of behavior that lead us to act morally and ethically. People need to act in accordance with their behavioral value systems. When they don't, they feel uncomfortable. We all have some value system and behave according to it. Your system may be a hedonistic one, where the pleasure principle rules. One extreme of this principle is "If it feels good or gives me advantage, regardless of the consequences, I'll do it." Values emphasizing altruism and service, à la Mother Teresa, exemplify the other extreme. Most of us fall somewhere in between. The most efficient value system leads to behavior that produces a healthy lifestyle. A healthy lifestyle is defined as one consisting of physical, emotional, intellectual, social, and spiritual health. A healthy lifestyle is happier, because there is less stress and hostility.

In order to make decisions based on your value system, you have to know yourself. A clear understanding of your personal value system is useful in this regard. Knowledge of your personal value system will help you to understand others as well. You will also be in a better position to communicate about value-laden information without getting angry.

Your personal value system can create ethical stressors if it is in conflict with the decisions you make. For me, values are more than habitual behavior. They are internalized standards of excellence closer to what is commonly referred to as a conscience. Most of the time, we know right from wrong; but acting on this knowledge is the hard part. Our conscience may be correctly formed, lax, or overly scrupulous. An open-minded examination of your values will allow you to determine where you stand in this regard. It will also help you edit old memories of what standards ought to be. This can provide guidance in your efforts to update and add new information from other sources. The clarification process, in your mind, should include a reevaluation of moral beliefs that form the structure of your ethical values. If your morals conflict with your business ethics, you are vulnerable to unneeded tension. Anger is more likely to be present. Developing consistency between your moral sense of right and wrong and the secular, professional, and business ethics you work under will help stabilize your moods.

It is as Roy Disney said when asked after Walt's death, "Do you find it hard to make decisions now that Walt is gone?" Roy said, "No. When you know what your values are, and you make decisions based on your values, you will not go wrong. Of course, there are times when I want to make a different decision than what my values dictate, but I know that if I do, it will turn out wrong. So, you see, making decisions is not hard, if you respect your value system, your ethics."

Values may involve morals or be of a purely secular nature. Moral values deal with the rightness or wrongness of decisions. They are usually inspired by your spiritual beliefs. Mental health experts have no particular expertise in moral matters other than to encourage each of us to develop a strong spiritual belief system. We know that will contribute to greater levels of personal happiness. Research with people the world over has proven beyond a shadow of a doubt that people with a strong spiritual belief system are happier and healthier. Whatever moral system you subscribe to, attempting to live according to it will contribute to a healthier lifestyle.

Secular values are concerned with our preferences. They have nothing to do with moral convictions. An example of a secular value could involve a choice of food. Some like Italian, others prefer Chinese; neither choice implies moral superiority. In their classic work, *Values and Teaching* (1966), Raths, Harmin, and Simon identified seven criteria of a value. These criteria apply to secular values but they may help you to sort through your beliefs in either area. This process can also help you identify beliefs that trigger anger. This will allow you to decide more rationally whether the emotional cost of the belief is justified. These criteria include choosing freely, choosing from alternatives, choosing after thoughtful consideration of the consequences of each alternative, prizing and cherishing, publicly affirming, acting upon choices, and repeating them. The following value decision-making guidelines can prove helpful. Ask yourself these questions when making decisions that are of value importance:

1. Is my decision/action compatible with my goals, values, and expectations?
2. Does it feel right?
3. Where does the act ultimately lead?
4. What is the track record of others when making a similar decision? Or, what is my track record when making a similar decision?
5. By doing this, what am I saying about myself?

VALUE DECISION-MAKING FLOW CHART

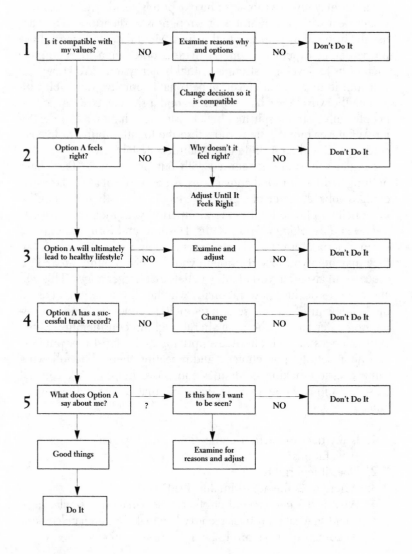

Value decision making is a dynamic process. The flow chart on the preceding page illustrates one method to assist your decision making. As you read through the chart Option A can stand for any action or decision you are trying to clarify.

When struggling to evaluate your decision-making processes, a matrix for examining your decisions may prove helpful. The guidelines contained in the matrix are based on the work of Sid Simon, Louis Raths and others, and can help you maintain consistency and clarity in your thinking when making important decisions. This is useful because your value system sometimes creates emotional blind spots. They can be troublesome when they lead you to give the benefit of the doubt to or to ignore activities others find objectionable.

Lindsay was torn between her desire to advance herself in the company and her personal convictions. Advancement could lead to more free time. The price of advancement was that she ignore company policy that she considered wrong. Lindsay considered her boss, Darryl, to be very self-oriented. If it worked for him, why worry about the consequences? One might say his values led to a rather lax conscience. Blind spots he experienced always provided him advantage, pleasure, or avoidance of personal responsibility for his actions. Blind spots cause some people to be overly scrupulous or perfectionistic. Darryl did not have to worry about that problem. Lindsay was struggling with a decision of whether or not to continue to work for a boss who promised rapid advancement but insisted that she ignore his unethical business practices.

People are able to communicate and problem solve more effectively when they recognize their own personal value system as well as the personal value systems of those they are dealing with. This realization prompted Lindsay to use the matrix that follows to think through her values a bit more carefully. She listed unethical business practices on the first line of the matrix.

Karen was a very strong supporter of Sonja's gymnastics, but was troubled by the method chosen to help junior athletes make weight. She was dying to have Sonja on the elite gymnastics team, so she listed "weight loss" in the matrix.

Linda's community service activities were taking too much time from her family. She put community service in the matrix. Complete the matrix with other areas of value concerns that are relevant to your circumstances.

DECISION-MAKING MATRIX							
DECISIONS/SITUATIONS	1	2	3	4	5	6	7
UNETHICAL BUSINESS PRACTICES	7	6	5	6	7	7	5
WEIGHT LOSS							
COMMUNITY SERVICE							

For each decision/situation included in the matrix above, circle the number below that best describes *you* in the decision process and enter the number on the horizontal axis of the box.

1. Was my decision freely made?
   Freely Made   1   2   3   4   5   6   7   Forced to Make

2. Do I like the position taken?
   Yes   1   2   3   4   5   6   7   No

3. Have I evaluated the pros and cons?
   Yes   1   2   3   4   5   6   7   No

4. Does this option have a successful track record in my experience?
   Yes   1   2   3   4   5   6   7   No

5. Is this decision in accordance with my values, attitudes, and beliefs?
   Yes   1   2   3   4   5   6   7   No

6. Will I stand up and publicly affirm this decision?
       Yes 1 2 3 4 5 6 7 No
7. Have I made a personal commitment to this course of action?
       Yes 1 2 3 4 5 6 7 No

INTERPRETATION ANSWERING SCALE

If the decision you are considering has answering scale values that mostly lie between 1 and 4, then you are probably making decisions that will promote a healthy lifestyle. If your answering scale values mostly lie between 5 and 7, as in the first one given (unethical business practices), you are probably making decisions that will promote an unhealthy lifestyle, add greater stress, and increase the risk of hostility. Now, what do your answers tell you about your decision-making procedure?

I learned that _____

I relearned that _____

I have a concern about _____

Lindsay decided that the personal price of moving up in this company was too high. She knew she could not be happy even with more money and better hours if she had to compromise her values. Surprisingly, once she made the decision, she immediately felt a huge sense of relief. She was reminded of a quote she had read in *The One Minute Manager*, by Kenneth Blanchard and Spencer Johnson, "People who feel good about themselves produce good results." It became easier for her to get her résumé together and hire an employment service. Before long, she had several attractive job offers. She realized that she had been emotionally stuck, that her work situation was draining a lot of her energy and a great deal of her goodwill. The decision to leave, more than anything else, helped her self-talk assume a much more positive tone. "I'm stuck, there is nothing I can do" changed to "There are alternatives, I can choose among them." As she continued to exercise her new sense of freedom, Lindsay realized that she was beginning to experience what

Steven Covey refers to as "the essence of effective time and life management."

She had begun to organize her life from a basis of balance and priorities. The basic problem for most people is that they fail to identify with their priorities. In Covey's words, "The basic problem is that their priorities have not become deeply implanted in their hearts and minds." It was comforting for Lindsay to know that she had changed that for herself.

The next step in her life-management plan was to decide on what pressing matters were really important and what pressing matters could wait. She decided to place her energies on the important matters of the day. Ones that were immediately urgent included the care and nurture of her children, getting to work on time, and the care and nurture of herself. The important issues of her life that were not urgent, but would have an important impact on her options in the not too distant and long-term future, needed attention as well. These included asking her employer about the possibility of leave time and financial support to complete the thirty credits needed for her B.S. degree. Doing her best to avoid urgent but unimportant phone calls would be another part of her new attitude. Multiple minor demands and gossip time were usually counterproductive anyway.

For the foreseeable future, Lindsay decided that anything that was not urgent and important was not worth her time. Focus would be in the areas that she had decided were urgent and important now. She would give more serious thought to identifying her key roles in life. Goals she selected would have to follow the One Minute Manager maxim "Always make sure that it is clear what your responsibilities are and what you are being held accountable for." Lindsay also made sure she identified her areas of accountability, responsibility, and authority for any goal that she committed herself to.

She would take the advice of management experts and keep the number of goals down. The 80–20 goal-setting rule made perfect sense to her. *The One Minute Manager* insists that 80 percent of the really important results will come from only 20 percent of our goals. By keeping that rule in mind, dropping unproductive activities was much easier, freeing up time for the activities she valued.

As she continued thinking through her life-management system, Lindsay vowed to "take a minute, look at her goals, look at her performance, and see if her behavior matched her goals" (*The One Minute Manager*).

Lindsay used her C.O.O.L. tools to project herself ahead to a conference with her boss. She mentally worked her way through the tough spots of the meeting well before she got there. It helped her, as well, to keep Covey's five important points in mind when it comes to self-management.

First, be principle centered. This empowered her by allowing her to view her time in the context of what was really important to her.

Second, your morals do matter, so be conscience directed. By clarifying her values, she made it easy to stick with this notion. The memories of the freedom and peace she felt the day she decided that her personal morals and ethics were more important than advancement helped a lot here.

Third, define your unique mission to include values and long-term goals. This gave her the energy to speak to her new boss and to mentally rehearse what it would take for her to have that meeting.

Fourth, balance your life by identifying roles and by setting goals and scheduling activities in each key role every week. This allowed Lindsay to combine motherhood, career advancement, and a little time for exercise.

Fifth, as with the first principle of C.O.O.L. parenting, be aware of the context in which you create your goals and management system. Weekly organization with daily adaptations has helped Lindsay get beyond the limiting perspective of a single day. The regular review of her key roles helps to keep her in touch with what is most important to her at this time in her life. You can do the same.

PART TWO

THE CHILD

CHAPTER 13

Modifying Behavior

One thing that parents of impulsive kids know is that their fears for their children's safety are real. The impulsive nature of these children places them at risk. They are ill-equipped to anticipate danger. The possible consequences of their actions don't deter them because "possible" doesn't seem to exist for these daring children. To make matters worse, they do not respond well to instructions either.

In order to influence Justin's behavior, Luke and Mary had to change their way of thinking about parenthood. It was becoming more and more obvious that love was not going to be nearly enough. They began to notice that Justin didn't remember instructions as well as the other boys in his play group. He was affectionate, his heart was in the right place, but somehow he just didn't pick up on social cues as quickly as the others did. He couldn't take a hint. They began to suspect that they would have to be much more consistent. They decided that in order to keep some semblance of sanity in the Costa family a more scientific approach to parenting would have to be developed. This went along with some of the reading they were doing and a documentary they saw about dealing with distractible children. Luke was guardedly optimistic as he expressed his hopes for his son's future. "We are trying to put in place systematic ways of influencing Justin's behavior. By observing the results of the things we try and modifying our plans accordingly, we hope that Justin will start to catch on like the girl in the documentary on impulsive children did.

"We know scolding, yelling, and nagging don't work. In fact, nagging may actually increase some of his undesirable behavior." Luke was also concerned with how Justin's problems were going to affect his younger sister Jessica. She seemed to get very fussy when he or Mary got mad at Justin. By the time Justin was five, it was becoming

135

obvious that reasoning didn't work with him when he got upset. "Is our child becoming addicted to negative attention?" Mary wondered.

As they learned more about influencing impulsive behavior, Luke and Mary realized that reinforcement does work. But parents sometimes, unknowingly, strengthen behavior they find objectionable. This happens when parents give too much attention to their children when they are behaving objectionably. Thus, parents reinforce bad behavior. Mary used to have confidence that her ideas of how children and parents should behave were on track. Now she wasn't so sure. It seemed as if everything she tried worked for a little while but soon became ineffective. This was very frustrating. She had to stop the triggering mechanism, but how?

Consider the case of the rainy day. Kids are indoors. The noise level is escalating. You remind them to use their inside voices when they're in the house. You suggest some more appropriate behavior, some quiet alternative to the noise they were making. For example, you might suggest that they work together on a puzzle rather than playing Power Rangers in the dining room.

Maybe they cooperate and get quiet. If so, give them a hug, offer some cookies, and thank them for using their quiet, inside voices. But if you are reading this book, you probably feel as if you have been through similar scenes many times before. You already know that immediate compliance in a situation like this is not very likely. Something will have to be done!

What should a C.O.O.L. parent do? Take your TEMPERature for starters. As you are planning your next move, take some time to consider your beliefs about what children "should" do. Although past behavior is the best predictor of future behavior, those thoughts "I have been through this a thousand times before," "I know I'm not likely to get compliance," "Something will have to be done" may become anger triggers in this situation. What you know to be true from the past can provoke anger in the present. Particularly if these triggers are hooked into unrealistic beliefs about what adults or children should or shouldn't do in a given situation.

Dr. Karen Horney, a famous psychoanalyst, wrote long ago about the tyranny of the "should." She observed that we are all raised to believe certain behavior, certain feelings, and certain thoughts are to be expected and others ought not to occur in certain situations. We develop these notions of should and ought as a result of our experiences in life. Our parents' beliefs are most important in molding our notion of what should and ought to be. Certainly we all need a code of conduct to live by, but angry adults take it so far that their anger gets stimulated when other emotions might serve them better.

To minimize her chances of being victimized by shoulds and oughts, Mary decided to take a closer look at the beliefs that raise her TEMPERature. She made a list of five shoulds and oughts that caused unwanted anger on a regular basis. She did this by reviewing her most Forgettable Flare-ups. The next time you get caught inside with a houseful of kids, perhaps your revised notion of what should or ought to be will help stabilize your emotions. Doing so made Mary less of a perfectionist. This will make your use of systematic consequences much more effective also. Your C.O.O.L. demeanor will eliminate any chance of inadvertently providing negative attention to the undesirable or dangerous behavior you are hoping to decrease. After you C.O.O.L. down with the anger-management techniques you have been practicing, you are ready to ACT!

Use one of the two techniques I'm going to describe for you now to decrease unacceptable behavior. The first, Time Out, is especially useful for younger children, up to the age of seven or eight. The second technique, which I have named the Thinking Zone, is suitable for older children because it requires specific activities designed to encourage children to think before they act.

The purpose of both Time Out and the Thinking Zone is to remove the child from the situation that is contributing to the development of unacceptable behavior. Time Out and the Thinking Zone also stimulate thinking. They help the child anticipate the consequences of his or her behavior more consistently and to build self-esteem. Children need the security of knowing limits will be established by parents. Consistency builds their sense of trust in self and you. Prepare yourself to guide their emerging autonomy in a way that promotes healthy growth and development.

We want to remove the child from a situation because we believe the situation is causing the child to develop bad habits. This happens if the situation provides reinforcement for unacceptable behavior. When Quentin was aggressively teasing his little brother, Jason, both children were suffering. The little brother was squealing in fear because he was unable to defend himself. Quentin felt powerful because he was in control. These feelings are huge payoffs that encourage domineering behavior. We want to stop the payoffs, in this case Jason's submissive behavior in response to Quentin's bullying ways.

Time Out is a method of weakening undesirable behavior. It is most useful with behavior that occurs frequently. Time Out is most effective when used in combination with a plan to strengthen desirable behavior. The desirable behavior you plan to strengthen should be an incompatible alternative to the objectionable behavior.

Time Out is a term often heard in discussions about working with difficult children. Unfortunately, it isn't very well understood, especially by many parents. When parents or professionals say "time out" they usually mean a place where a child is sent as punishment. When I say "time out" what I mean is a period of time during which the child is removed from the opportunity to be reinforced. Time Out has to do with a relationship, not a location. If you and I are talking and I walk away, leaving you alone, that puts you in Time Out. Your behavior, talking, is no longer being reinforced by my behavior, listening.

So what are the rules for the appropriate use of Time Out? First, use Time Out only for certain, specified behaviors. Most parents find it useful to develop a list of negative behavior. Select five aspects of your child's behavior that you want to decrease. Arrange them in order according to your estimate of how difficult they will be to change. Begin with one of the easier ones.

Children of different ages have different perceptions of time. Be prepared to back up the requirement that the child must be quiet *before* he or she may leave the area. Occasionally, this may take up to one or two hours. The child may be noisy so long as he or she does not leave the chair. The Time Out will continue until the child has been quiet in the chair for a short time, ten to twenty seconds will do. When the child realizes you mean business, he or she will almost always quiet down quickly by the second or third "extra innings" Time Out. When the Time Out is over, the child must do whatever he or she was asked to do originally, or return to the Time Out area. If the behavior involved an impulsive act, such as name calling or hitting, the child must be willing to apologize and promise not to do it again. If the child refuses, tell him or her to stay in Time Out until he or she is told to come out. The sequence begins all over. Establish your own guidelines based on your child and his or her response to the consequence. Consider also the specific problem behavior you know you are likely to encounter with your child. Other possibilities might include teasing, playing with food, arguing with you.

The important thing is to be consistent within the bounds you have set for your child. Identify the behavior you want your child to exhibit in place of the undesirable behavior. Develop a plan to encourage the positive alternative behavior. For example: If Eric's teasing of Kelly is driving you crazy, develop a plan to strengthen cooperation, pleasant words, and supportive actions. Be sure to explain what you are doing and why—once! It helps your child understand that you mean business if you put the plan in writing.

Focus on the good behavior you hope to increase. I call that good behavior the acceleration target. Speaking kindly to each other, sharing toys, and watching TV together without fighting are examples of acceleration targets.

Cooperative Behavior Plan the purpose of which is to increase cooperative play between Eric and Kelly.

Positive Consequences
Reinforce both children for

1. Speaking kindly to each other.
2. Sharing toys.
3. Watching TV together.

Negative Consequences
Time Out

1. 10 minutes for arguing.
2. 10 minutes for hitting.

The timer will be started immediately after the child is seated in the designated Time Out area.

How long in Time Out? The least amount of time that is effective is a good rule of thumb. For preschoolers, one minute per year of age is a good starting place. For school-age children, make it two minutes per year of age.

Remember, Time Out procedures are designed to be brief if the child complies. Here's what you do:

1. Take your TEMPERature. Once you are sure you are ready, take action, enter the area where the child is.
2. Label the behavior as inappropriate. State the contingency in a matter-of-fact manner, without sounding as if you're upset. In other words, don't yell and don't beg. For example, "Eric, teasing Kelly is inappropriate behavior. You have a choice. Treat Kelly kindly or go to Time Out for ten minutes. You have thirty seconds to decide." Walk away and observe. If the teasing stops, praise Eric for playing cooperatively with Kelly. If he continues to tease her, say, "Eric, go to Time Out now."
3. Provide an opportunity for the child to go unassisted to the Time Out area.

   A NOTE ABOUT LOCATION: It is generally best to use a specific chair in a specific place. It could be in any boring area that is free of distractions, away from other people, and free of danger. Avoid using the child's room if possible. A chair placed in the hallway works well. DO NOT USE a dark closet or any other space that would frighten the child. It should be a well-lit ventilated space. Your objective is to provide a safe haven which eliminates the reinforcement for inappropriate behavior, not to terrify your child. Fear tactics do get quick results at first. Unfortunately, they have lots of terrible side effects if used too often. The use of fear leads to very unpredictable long-term results. As children outgrow a fear tactic, you must increase the level of aversiveness to get the same result. Children often get hurt physically and emotionally in the process.
4. If your child balks, physically take him or her there immediately. Use the least amount of force required to accomplish your goal. If the child leaves the chair, confront him or her immediately and use physical restraint. Physical restraint by the parent means using the *least* amount of force necessary to gently but firmly keep the child in the chair. Calmly explain that the child will be allowed to leave when the child has served his or her time.
5. Start timing as soon as the child is in the appropriate place and behaving acceptably.

6. As soon as the required time has been met, return the child at once to a reinforcing activity. Then go about your business as if the entire incident never happened.

On the following pages, I've included a description of this procedure in action.

If Eric is teasing his sister Kelly, while Mom's temperature is rising, Mom's initial response should include three steps:

1. Awareness—make the child aware of the instruction verbally. Mom says, "Kids, play cooperatively or go to separate rooms." After a brief pause (five to ten seconds), assuming Eric keeps teasing,
2. Mom touches Eric's shoulder and makes eye contact as she gives him his one and only reminder. Mom says, "Eric, it's your choice, play cooperatively or go to Time Out now."
3. At this point, Eric may choose to play cooperatively. If he starts teasing again, tell him to go to Time Out immediately. If he chooses to go directly, he will spend ten minutes in Time Out and return to playing only after he has completed his "sentence." He must end it with ten to twenty seconds of silence. He must apologize to Kelly. A promise to play cooperatively or choose another activity is also required. If he rebels and refuses to go to Time Out, Mom says, "You choose. Go to Time Out at once or have five minutes added to your time."

If Eric cooperates, he will spend ten minutes, otherwise he will serve his original ten minutes plus an additional five minutes before returning to play. If Eric balks, Mom physically escorts him to Time Out, using the least amount of force necessary to get him there. As soon as the required time has been completed, and an apology has been given, she allows Eric to return to play. If the temper tantrum continues while in Time Out, Mom continues the Time Out until Eric quiets down for a few seconds. She does not dwell on the misdeed. She lets it pass. She says nothing more about it!

The length of time spent in either Time Out or the Thinking Zone is not what makes these techniques so valuable. What makes them effective is the fact that they are immediate, consistent, and inescapable. One thing that often happens with Time Out is that the child is so agitated and so angry that he or she continues to complain, to stomp, and to disrupt the environment. WHAT DO YOU DO? Ignore the noise, but observe unobtrusively until the child is quiet. If the child starts to leave the chair, stands, knocks the chair over, or moves the chair more than a foot, intervene immediately. Begin your intervention by taking your TEMPERature. Mentally reviewing an outline of your Three Act Play will help you defuse anger during this procedure. Once you are in the Action Zone:

1. Get down on the child's level.
2. Make eye contact.
3. Clap your hands loudly and directly in front of the child's face. DO NOT HIT THE CHILD.
4. Say in a very firm voice, "You will stay in Time Out until I tell you to leave."
5. Move away from the child and observe unobtrusively.
6. If the child attempts to leave again, repeat the procedure one more time.
7. If the child attempts to leave the chair a third time, use physical restraint as described above.
8. If you can't remain calm, place the child in a safe area until you regain your composure. Professional consultation is recommended if this happens more than once.

I do not recommend spanking, because angry parents often underestimate their anger level and hit too hard or lose control and hit too often. Spanking is subject to the same problems as other aversive procedures. I would never support a government ban on spanking, however, simply because the cure would be worse than the problem.

If spanking is your preference, do it like this. With authority and conviction, tell the child that if he or she leaves the chair before the time is up, *"you will be spanked!"* I do not recommend spanking for children who are over ten years of age. If the child leaves the chair again, put him or her over your knee and strike the child two normal spanks with the open hand on the buttocks. Do not remove clothing or strike with a belt, spoon paddle, or other object.

If spanking is unacceptable to you, identify a safe space that allows you to enforce Time Out. Remove all toys, television and so on, from the child's room and have the child stay there. Decide in advance what to do if the child tries to leave the room. Loss of TV, bike, or other privileges should be considered in this case. If your child does not respond to these procedures after one month of consistent application, seek professional assistance. Sooner is better than later if the behavior is getting worse. The same is true if you are having difficulty with self-control. If the child is believed to be physically dangerous to himself or others, he or she should be evaluated by a psychologist, psychiatrist, or other mental health professional immediately.

Now let's talk about the Thinking Zone. As I mentioned earlier, the Thinking Zone is generally more appropriate for older children. They have the ability, whether they want to use it or not, to think about their improper behavior in an analytical way. The beginning steps you will take with the Thinking Zone are identical to the ones that you use with Time Out. Turn back a couple of pages to review Steps 1 through 6 now if you need to.

Where the two approaches differ dramatically, and importantly, is in what the child does while he or she is in the designated area. While in the Thinking Zone, the older child will be asked to write a report, giving his or her side of the story. Ask the child to include what he or she thinks your side of the story is. Also, require an opinion about the incident from the perspective of whoever else was involved, such as a brother or sister. Make sure the child completes the writing assignment. The child must include his or her own suggestions about appropriate behavior under similar circumstances in the future. Remember, to be effective, the Thinking Zone must require the child to participate actively in owning and solving the problem behavior. Problem ownership requires that the child verbalize his or her responsibility for the actions and apologize. The child must also suggest a solution.

I've included a modified version of a form that I have used for years. You may make copies of this form if you wish, or devise a similar form of your own. Keep it simple and use it consistently.

THINKING ZONE REPORT FORM

Date: _____　　Time: _____　　Location: _____

CHILD TO COMPLETE

1. My explanation of what happened:

_____

_____

_____

2. What I think others believe happened:

_____

_____

_____

3. How I plan to handle similar situations appropriately in the future:

_____

_____

_____

Action taken:

_____

_____

If you would like to use the Thinking Zone concept with younger children who may not be able to write well enough to handle the form, let them use a tape recorder to report the incident and their thoughts about it. Kids love to talk on tape recorders!

Again, the purpose is to reinforce in the child the development of foresight, judgment, and self-esteem. The prevention of future problems is the objective. By learning to think ahead and anticipate the consequences of his or her behavior, your child should become better able to make healthy choices. This will allow you to interact in a loving, positive way with your child, rather than become frustrated and angry yourself. Unlike putting a child on restriction, which often involves consequences that continue for days or weeks, the Thinking Zone aims to provide almost immediate opportunity to strengthen the correct set of responses. That's why we have the child rejoin an activity after a short absence.

Your purpose is to stop the payoff. The choice of whether the child thinks or not is the child's. Your can't stop the child from tearing up his or her room, if that's the child's choice.

You can't stop the child from thinking angry thoughts, if that's the child's choice.

You can't stop the child from yelling and screaming, if that's the child's choice.

You CAN keep your C.O.O.L. and give no hint of anger.

You can keep the child in the Thinking Zone.

You can require that the child make restitution for damaged goods, clean the disrupted area plus another room, complete the original directive, and promise to do better in the future.

To stop the payoff, you must play by the rules most of the time. The rule is, the child cannot come out until he or she has spent the required amount of time and completed the writing assignment. The timer starts immediately upon the child's entering the Time Out location.

Of course, you will have to exercise your own judgment in many cases. Make sure the child understands the rule before it is applied. Remember, your goal is to build goodwill even when it hurts. These two procedures work best to decrease misbehavior that occurs frequently. Longer periods of restriction work better for older children who occasionally break serious rules.

Try to use working restrictions when misbehavior involves financial loss. In other words, have your child earn the money to make restitution. I would consider lost wages a financial cost. When you must take time off and lose money or annual leave to attend school conferences for disciplinary reasons more than once a marking period — charge! A sliding scale for your lost time will make an impression. This approach is most effective for preadolescents or adolescents. The hourly fee is largely symbolic. But it will help establish the "if, then" connection. If you select choice A, then you will experience consequence B. Forethought and self-talk are the essence of impulse control so necessary for judgment. An hourly fee based on minimum wage will let your child know your time is valuable and not to be taken for granted. A ratio of two hours payback for each hour of pay or vacation lost is reasonable.

It is very important that you are fair in this regard. Allen was taunted and threatened by a group of bullies in the eighth grade. When he finally defended himself, he was suspended along with the bullies for fighting. Allen had no history of fighting, and his conduct grades were Bs and Cs. While suspended, Allen was not allowed to complete missed assignments, which meant he received a 0 for one-sixth of the marking period. I consider this school policy unreasonable. I would encourage you to work to change such policies if they exist in your school. School board policies are often very sensitive to political power brokers in the area. I urge parents to participate in the democratic process. Let the school board, principal, and teacher know about your objections. Lobby school boards to change what you consider unreasonable rules. If you investigate and advocate, your child will gain increased respect for your rules and won't contest them as often. The degree to which you discipline your child for infractions and rules you consider unreasonable is a matter of conscience and family values. If a child has failing grades, plan regular two-to-three-hour periods of study time per night. Do this five or six nights a week until the report card improves. Our community has a number parents may call for homework assignments. If your child has always struggled to make grades, a comprehensive psychoeducational evaluation should be completed to find out why school is so difficult. This evaluation should take place as soon as the problem is detected, not six or seven months into the school year. Children with conduct problems as well as academic problems should be thoroughly evaluated by a psychologist also. Use tutors as needed. Your child should do chores to pay for part of the tutoring if it results from a negative attitude. If your child's behavior is beyond your ability to cope with, seek professional help, especially if your child is becoming overly aggressive or you doubt your ability to control your level of response. If you believe you are a danger to yourself or to your child, call 911 for help immediately.

A psychologist or mental health professional can make a big difference in the quality of your life. If you don't know how to ask for such help, speak to your family doctor, clergyman or your child's guidance counselor. Some doctors and clergy are reluctant to recommend, or will advise against, psychological help. I would change doctors or churches if you run into this outdated thinking.

The local psychological association can be a resource. The National Register of Health Service Providers in Psychology is an excellent resource for identifying qualified professionals. Ignore slick advertising campaigns; they usually mean that business is bad. Ask for proof of qualifications. Ask friends and professionals for a referral. CHADD, the support group for families of children with ADD and ADHD, is also an excellent resource. The mental health association in your community can also provide information.

If your child refuses to participate in family counseling and is acting out in ways that are illegal or dangerous, involve the juvenile court. For some, this is the only way to get their attention. If conflicts approach the point of physical violence, call the police. Remember, the longer the hostile words continue, the greater the chance that family violence will erupt. Don't get trapped in physical or verbal power struggles with older children or teens who are ready to physically fight with you. Get control by calling for backup. All of my experiences of getting police and juvenile court involved have been positive. That action has either brought the pubescent youngster under control or contributed directly to a much needed reality check that did. Unfortunately, not every family has a happy ending to report. But doing this will give you the satisfaction of knowing that you did all you could to provide proper guidance.

If you have a child with ADHD, ADD, or other significant problems, select insurance coverage that has good mental health benefits. You will need them. If yours doesn't, change it or lobby for change.

High-maintenance kids require much more money as well as energy. Skilled help is needed for their many problems. If you are divorced, your child support should reflect these needs. The costs of not treating oppositional and defiant offspring are extremely high. Getting your family and child competent professional help can be an excellent investment in more ways than one. An aggressive or depressed child is much more likely to join a deviant subculture or get involved with drugs and illegal or dangerous activities. The logical consequences of this chain of events include low self-esteem and poor vocational skills. Ultimately, such children are more likely to get arrested, pregnant, injured, or only marginally employed. The resulting legal or medical costs alone can be staggering. The personal costs of supporting and worrying about a marginally employable young adult can be heartbreaking as well as financially draining.

The cost of getting your family help by a trained professional is about the same as braces for their teeth. The choice of what to straighten out and when is not always an easy one, but you do have a choice.

CHAPTER 14

Enforcing Discipline

"Do I have to do it, Mom?"

"I hate you, Mom!"

"In a little while, Mom . . ."

You've probably heard all three of those statements whined, yelled, moaned, and bellowed by your child—more times than you care to remember. So how do you respond? If you are like most of us, you probably scold, lecture, or smack the child. The purpose of parenthood is to produce successors, and ideally, improve them. Most of the parents I know believe they have a moral and social duty to teach their children right from wrong. It has been my experience that the majority of parental anger results from attempts to perform this duty correctly, in the vernacular of days gone by, to fulfill the duties of their state in life.

I believe punishment has an important place in child rearing. Unfortunately, much of what passes for punishment, isn't! Almost 75 percent of American parents spank their children. They believe they are teaching right from wrong by doing so. More often than not, they are teaching their children to fear the raised hand but ignore their calmly spoken words. They are actually teaching their children to disrespect them. Most parents wait entirely too long to make a decisive response to objectionable behavior. The child learns to ignore their words until their mom or dad is really angry. After a while, some even ignore the anger. This happens because anger may be loud, unpleasant, and harmful to the self-esteem of the giver and receiver, but it is *not* punishment. Punishment has nothing to do with pain. The only way to know if what you have done to your child has punished him or her is to note its impact on the behavior it was designed to reduce. If it reduced the behavior, then it was punishment. If it didn't, then it wasn't punishment.

Sometimes yelling and hitting actually increase objectionable behavior. In that case, you are reinforcing, not punishing, it. To be effective, punishment must be immediate, contingent, or clearly connected to the misbehavior, and inescapable. The size of the punishment is less important than its immediacy. Punishment is most effective when it is used with positive reinforcement. Angry parents often fail to understand that their ranting may actually be increasing the very behavior they want to stop, because their children know they can ignore it. That's what their body language is teaching their children. Speak quietly and follow through consistently, especially when teaching something new. Children can freeze if you scare them too often. The confusion and anxiety they feel will make it much more difficult for them to answer your questions. Don't let that trigger even more anger on your part. Some kids get so good at hiding their fear and confusion, they should get an award. Unfortunately, you do not get the feedback that would stop you. In fact, you may misread their stoicism as defiance. Be careful about that. The result of learning to stuff feelings is not positive.

ADHD children have a documented deficit in language. This deficit is so pronounced that a simple word association test may predict ADHD almost as precisely as many sophisticated neuropsychological assessment batteries. The test merely asks the child to name all the words he or she can think of that begin with a certain letter, such as L, and allows the child one minute to do so. Can you imagine how intimidating direct questioning can be to a child who has this problem? I bet you can, because ADHD is so likely to be inherited that if your child has it, there is a good chance that you or your spouse had the same problem.

Learn to avoid the twenty questions anger trap when trying to get your child to tell you something. Your child's inability to provide you with a snappy reply may be a result of his or her problem with expressive language, not defiance. Normal kids balk, too. Anxiety will cause anyone's fluency to get messed up.

The look in your eyes, your tone of voice, and your overall physical demeanor are more important than the words you select, particularly when instructing or disciplining your child. How you say what's on your mind will go a long way in determining the reaction you get. Mary had discovered that her responses to these invitations to anger fell into one of four categories: ignoring, escalating, venting all her frustrations inappropriately, or dealing directly with the situation at hand. When your child gets rude or disrespectful, it gets very easy to respond in kind. As Mary considered the feelings that were aroused inside of her, she remembered that she could get away with ignoring some of this behavior, but if she ignored too much for too long, she wound up feeling frustrated and irritated. Mary had learned that she could increase her self-control by rating her anger level. She was getting pretty comfortable handling some of the cooler crises, the ones that sparked low- or mid-range tension. Those upper-end problems still prompted her to get right down on her child's level and let the child have it. Especially if Mary was really tired, upset, or generally not feeling well. She was beginning to realize that keeping track of her Success Stories as well as her Forgettable Flare-ups was also helping her to understand the context in which the escalation occurred. It also helped her to *post reminders to deal with situations directly*. Techniques that were successful for her in the past could sometimes be forgotten in the heat of an angry exchange.

Aggression among intimates normally occurs at the end of a sequence of aversive events. I learned long ago that people like Mary need to deal with the links in their chain of anger very early in the sequence. During the years 1972 through 1974, I did a great deal of work with very aggressive adolescents. My staff at the Hospital School at Woodward, Iowa, had the patience of saints. These were some of the finest people I've ever worked with. But they were everyday people just like you. They had to learn how to deal with the emotions these severely aggressive kids triggered. About the same time, Dr. Gerald Patterson of the Oregon Social Learning Center was pioneering the systematic examination of social interaction sequences. He discovered that behavior of hostile families was not so dissimilar from what we were discovering in our intensive treatment unit.

Aggression follows chains of aversive interactions. Some of the more abrasive people that you work or socialize with probably exhibit similar signals. They send out many invitations to anger. Fortunately, most are ignored. The sequence of events that lead to your most Forgettable Flare-ups occurs in brief blips. Only a couple of seconds pass by. Most of the time, we ignore abrasive behavior, provocative comments, or sarcasm, and they go away. That's why awareness of the context, being prepared to breathe, reduce body tension, and counteract triggering thoughts by communicating with yourself is so important. In effect, these actions distract you long enough to disarm the triggering mechanism. They substitute for the normal response of ignoring the provocative comment.

Dr. Patterson has discovered numerous triggers that stimulate aggressive behavior. Many are nonverbal, such as voice inflection, volume, or other voice qualities. A contemptuous, sarcastic tone, for example, clearly is provocative. But other forms of sarcasm put up barriers to intimacy and often go unnoticed. The put-down tone can either be provocative as a trigger or laughed off as a humorous comment, depending on the context. Coldness in the voice, whining, certainly snarling and loud, harsh voice qualities are clearly attempts to intimidate, which sometimes trigger angry responses. Sounds that you might make, such as sighing and groaning, can also trigger reactions, as can ultimatums—"Do this or else"—or guilt trips—"After all I've done for you"—and accusations—"You did it again, didn't you?" Profanity, insults, dismissing comments such as "Get out of here," expletives, and direct threats—"Back off or I'll beat your butt"—are potent triggers. Blaming, humiliating comments such as "Are you really that stupid or are you just putting up a good act?" and feigning innocence—"Oh, I didn't realize the mud on the carpet would offend you"—are troublemakers. "I know what you're thinking" is a kind of mind-reading provocation that reveals assumptions you are making about the person to whom you are speaking. Your interpretations, which may or may not be correct, increase tension in either case. Simply refusing to respond—"I have nothing more to say"—a stonewalling technique, or complaining and overgeneralizing—"You are never happy with anything"—will aggravate. Even giving advice can be provocative—"Ask your father. He knows you need more money for a new pair of shoes."

Teasing is a much more provocative behavior than many of us realize. Many adults don't realize how much they tease little children. Since young children think in concrete terms, teasing is often misunderstood by them. They are frequently confused or frustrated by adult humor at their expense. Children are easy to excite. An adult so easily influences a child's emotions that teasing can have a powerful attraction to the insecure adult. Perhaps that is one of the reasons why teasing is so common among siblings. Of course, physical gestures, such as pointing a finger, shaking a fist, flipping a bird, folded arms across the chest, and a whole host of other behaviors are also potent nonverbal anger triggers.

Human attention is one of the most powerful influences on the mind, body, and behavior. Use your attention wisely. What are some of the ways your body language communicates? How about your body posture or your facial expressions? Consult your Forgettable Flare-ups to help you remember menacing aspects of your demeanor. You might want to review your Flare-ups in a family forum on what your body language has meant to others. Can you think of any of your habitual ways of presenting yourself that could be perceived as an attack? Write down several in the spaces below:

_____

_____

_____

We all have a comfort zone for physical space, words, and gestures. Entering another's physical space or boundary is provocative. Try this simple exercise to discover how close is comfortable, close enough, and provocative for each of your family members.

Stand on opposite sides of a room. Pair up with different family members facing one another. One person will remain in position while the other walks to him or her. Flip a coin to see who walks first. Walk toward your partner until your partner says stop to indicate when he or she feels you are close enough. The person who is defining a comfort zone will tell you when you are a comfortable distance, or too close for their comfort. Comfort zones decrease when negative responses are anticipated and increase in anticipation of affection.

You and your children might find it interesting to play the Comfort Zone Game. You can do this by defining comfort zones while role-playing different emotional scenarios or repeating the same scenario with different family members. For example, pretend you

(Mom or Dad) or a sibling are approaching them to see report cards when they are happy about showing you a good report card, worried about showing a marginal report card, or ashamed of showing a failing report card to various family members.

There are many ways to break up the aversive chains of verbal and nonverbal behavior. The first, of course, is to not buy into the chain at all. Taking time to chill out and leave the situation was described earlier, and it is appropriate to consider it again now.

A good faith contract between your child and yourself can work very well to make truces and time-out more effective. As early as third grade, perhaps even sooner for some children, this technique works very well. Contracting has a long history of success as a self-control strategy. It allows all involved to feel a part of the process of productive response generation. It invites healthy feelings of power and value. These are often damaged in families used to escalating anger. When reprogramming anger and aggression, a belief that you are valued and powerful combats the feelings of helplessness that parent-child power struggles are so good at creating.

A time-out contract emphasizes shared responsibility for the child. It can be used very effectively in combination with the Thinking Zone. It requires the ability to make a commitment to change patterns of behavior that are mutually painful. Children want to please their parents most of the time. Even the angry, provocative ones. Others are addicted to negative attention to such an extent that they have found aggravating you a much more reliable way of getting your attention than constructive approaches.

Gary discovered that a contract worked quite well with Quentin. The following outline is adapted from *When Anger Hurts* by Dr. Matthew McKay. Both parent and child must complete the contract for it to be most effective.

Behavior Contract:
    When I realize that my TEMPERature is rising, I will give a T sign for time-out, just like they do in the ball game. I will choose a ten-minute or one-hour time-out and leave the area at once. I promise not to hit or kick anything. I promise not to slam any doors.
    I will return no later than the stated time. I will take a walk, listen to music, or some other constructive action. I promise that

while I am away, I will try to keep positive thoughts in my mind. I will avoid focusing on the things that make me angry. When I return, I promise to start the conversation with "I know I was partly wrong and partly right." I will then admit to something that you said or did that was partly right. I will acknowledge something I said as partly wrong.

If you give me a T sign and leave, I will return the sign and let you go without a hassle, no matter what is going on. When you return, I will start the conversation with "I know I was partly wrong and partly right."

The time-out process will only work if good faith is clearly evident. If the process is abused, the contract will be voided.

Name: _____   Name: _____

Date: _____   Date: _____

Because time-out can be perceived by some parents as condoning disrespect, it is extremely important that you understand that the purpose of the interaction is not to allow the child to gain the upper hand. The purpose of the interaction is to allow problem solving to proceed. You, as a parent, are in no way required to give in to demands that you consider unreasonable. I am focusing on presenting a process of problem solving when angry that communicates your love and respect to your child. The message is clear that you are approachable even on important matters that sometimes make you mad. When they see that you are approachable, your children feel respected. As they begin to feel respected, their need to prove they can extract respect from you with power plays will be defused. As with other new habits, if you practice on little problems, the big ones will take care of themselves.

Another way of defusing angry exchanges is to validate the intensity of the feelings. As your voice volume increases or as you detect some other sign of hostility in yourself, you might use it as a cue. Remind yourself to own your emotions and validate them instead of arguing or responding with some other angry retort. You can do this by saying, "I'm feeling very angry right now" or "We both seem to be getting pretty upset, suppose we come back to this later."

If your son behaves rudely to you after getting off the phone with his girlfriend, as was the case in Tony's situation, try this approach. Simply state that "I couldn't help but overhear some harsh words between you and Megan. If you want to talk about it later, I'll be glad to listen." This indicates concern without criticizing. It could open the door to empathy and relationship building by ignoring the temptation to criticize the vocabulary. Tony chose not to punish or criticize Carl for his vocabulary. He thought, instead, that he would try to offer some support. Tony's empathetic hunch paid off later when Carl said, "I'm sorry for the language, Dad, but *Megan makes me so mad.*"

There are some other very important aspects to your communication that can help you to be more effective, particularly with the older children. The use of "I" statements, for example, can leave the door open to bonding opportunities. "You" statements are heard as much more accusatory. For example, Brenda is summoned to Josh's room by the shrill screams that tell her he is in deep trouble. The first thing that she sees is Quentin twisting Josh's arm back. Her Anger Awareness Journal indicates that she jumped right between the boys, grabbed Quentin by the hair, and yanked him back, as she screamed, "You are always beating up on your little brother. What's the matter with you? You are turning out to be a little monster, just like your father. Get out of here, I don't want to see you again. If you ever lay another hand on Josh, I am going to break it, do you hear me? Now, get to your room."

Later, review of the journal explained what happened. Josh's screams alarmed her. By the time she got to Josh's room, Brenda felt terrified. Her self-talk triggers included "I just know Josh's hurt." As she rushed to the room, she was thinking, "This kid is turning into a regular monster. I don't know what I am going to do with him. He is just like his father. What has he done to my baby this time?"

You can see from her inner dialog that she was priming herself for a Forgettable Flare-up. When she got to the room, her anger rush distorted her perception. She overestimated the physical risk to Josh. She played out the scene her trigger thoughts led her to believe she would find. She followed through. She made no effort to find out what was really going on, or even to give Quentin a chance to tell his side of the story. For his part, Quentin felt abandoned by his mother and humiliated. He was also scared stiff about what she might do to him. He was confused as to her reasons why. As far as he knew, he and Josh were just roughhousing. He hadn't even hurt Josh, but Mom, fearing the worst, jumped to conclusions. The wrong ones. When she sat down with Quentin later, Brenda was able to recognize that what she had been saying was wrong. She could have just blown it off, but instead she tried to make things right. She went into his room, sat with him for a while, and revealed some of her feelings.

"Quentin, I felt terrified when I heard your brother squealing. Would you mind telling me what you think he was yelling about?" Quentin replied, "I don't know, Mom. He was having fun. Maybe I was a little too rough, but he was laughing." The next time the squealing occurred, Brenda reacted differently. She cooled down, considered the context and consequences, objectively observed, organized options, and looked at herself as she wanted to be. As she walked slowly to the room, she thought to herself, "Calm down. Get all the facts before you accuse." She separated the two boys. Each was given two minutes to explain his side of the story. Her C.O.O.L. demeanor communicated a businesslike resolve that compelled Quentin and Josh's attention. Both related a reasonable story.

One of the most important things to avoid is trying to predict what another person is thinking. Sometimes my clients think I can read their minds. I often tell clients that "I do not have a crystal ball, I'm easy to fool." I say this for a particular purpose. Obviously I am trained in analyzing subtleties in communication, but I want those I am speaking with to assume responsibility for what they decide to say or withhold. Parents must sometimes become investigators. Particularly if they believe their children are involved in something illegal or very dangerous, but that is not what I am talking about here. I am talking about interrupting someone, denying that person the benefit of the doubt, or contradicting or calling that person a liar, based on what you believe or think that person "really" means. There may be an element of truth to what you believe; you may even be 100 percent correct in this particular situation. But to use this type of mind-reading or intuitive sense of what someone is thinking in a hostile, emotionally charged environment is a surefire way to provoke further escalation of a tense situation. If you are brainstorming with someone in an environment in which you are invited to give your opinions, do so freely. Intuition builds bridges here. In a tense situation, too much intuition burns them.

Lastly, avoid using the all-or-none words such as *always* or *never*. Overgeneralizing can be extremely provocative. A definite turnoff. It's rare that we *always* or *never* do anything. Very little in life is all or none and yet some of our most violent arguments are escalated by statements that claim or blame 100 percent. This type of overgeneralization has no place in the C.O.O.L. parent vocabulary. Dealing directly with the problem will go much further toward solving it.

If you know you have a tendency to behave in a demeaning or intimidating way, it is your responsibility to change. The Three Act Play can be very helpful in this regard. Review your Most Forgettable Flare-ups for some clues. Identify things you habitually do or say, or postures that you take that may be provocative. Use your Success Stories to remind you of nonverbal communication that builds bridges. Mentally rehearse those phrases, looks, distances, and voice qualities that invite understanding. Pay attention to the body language used by associates. Notice how some people have a knack for making you feel welcome. Notice the body language of actors in ad campaigns. Marketing psychology relies very heavily on body language to influence you. By being more aware of the body language of others, you will be more mindful of the messages your body is sending. Body language speaks much louder than words. Why not use it to your advantage? A better understanding of body language will help you to a deeper understanding of your children's communication as well. As you gain more confidence in your ability to project and read body language, you will naturally develop more confidence in your ability to be assertive rather than aggressive when it comes to limit-setting. When issuing instructions, your approach should be calm but resolute.

Use your imagery rehearsal to practice responding appropriately in any situation. If you are unsure of what you are doing that is provocative, ask. Ask someone you trust; even ask your children to tell you some of the things you do that make them defensive. Just about all kids are expert manipulators, heartstring tuggers, and guilt-button-pushers!

High-energy kids are especially adept at testing our limits with guilt trips, begging and bartering, and outright threats. Especially if you and your spouse or your mother-in-law don't agree on how to raise them. Why do they do this to you? Because they have so much practice! The very reason they get in trouble a lot is that they have so much energy and so little forethought. Remember, they don't learn rules well! They don't anticipate consequences. If you're going to be effective, it will take more than words. They must see the resolve in your eyes. When you ask your child to do something, be prepared to back up the request with consequences—positive or negative. Don't get into battles you can't win! If you can't back it up, don't ask!

Eye contact is crucial! Kneel down on one knee if necessary. State the request in a businesslike way, not as if you're asking a question or a favor. Use of the imperative will increase compliance by 30 percent even if you do nothing else. Be clear and give one instruction at a time. State the time frame in which you expect your child to complete the request. Set the stage for listening. For example, if the stereo is on, ask your son or daughter to turn it off, or turn it off yourself so your child can hear you. Be specific!

Instead of asking your child to clear the table after dinner, say, "Please put the dishes and silverware in the dishwasher." If you have a frequent problem with misunderstanding, write down the request, or have the child repeat the request back to you. For regular chores such as kitchen cleanup, you might post an index-card-size instruction sheet that states exactly what is to be done. Lists will improve performance for any task.

Job Description

Put dishes in dishwasher.
Wipe table with damp cloth.
Put away milk, bread, etc.
Return chairs under table.
Ask Mom or Dad to inspect within fifteen minutes of completing the meal.

Also state the time allowed for completion. If procrastination is a problem, set a time limit and get a timer. A portable kitchen timer works fine. In fact, this kind of simple timer works well as a reminder for many requests. Setting a time limit for compliance helps the child think ahead. And it will help both of you avoid arguments caused by you having to nag to get things done.

The timer gives a clear message without you saying a word. You announce, "Jamal, please clean up the kitchen. The list is on the refrigerator. You have sixty seconds to start and fifteen minutes to finish. Then you can watch Bart Simpson."

Start the timer.

What if he says, "But, Mom! Do I have to?" Tic . . . tic . . . tic . . . "Right after 'The Simpsons'!" Tic . . . tic . . . tic . . .

But there can be only one response for noncompliance. Shut off the TV. "No Simpsons tonight." Praise compliance, of course.

It is only fair to make the request in a timely manner so that your child has time to complete the task before a favorite program. And being allowed to view a favorite program after successful completion of a task reinforces his or her desire to complete the task.

Don't forget those all-important nonverbal forms of communication—smiles and hugs. They're great at helping to prevent or reverse negative addiction, so be generous with positive reinforcement.

CHAPTER 15

Reversing Bad Habits

"Stay C.O.O.L.?" you say. "But look at Jamal's room! It's a disaster! I talk to Jamal but he never seems to hear me. These kids are slobs. Why, most of them couldn't keep the neatness bug alive and well for a day." Sounds like your house?

Consider the overall situation—and simpify your life! How? The C.O.O.L. techniques can help you do it. Before you blow your top, consider the context and consequences of doing so, objectively observe yourself, organize your options for productive problem solving, and look to the future to envision how you would like to approach your child. Learning from your past mistakes will help you avoid making similar ones in the future. So start by giving instructions in a manner that is likely to be heard.

Many children have difficulty following directions. The reasons may include difficulties with maintaining attention or concentration, nervousness, or defiance. There are, of course, many other reasons why children might have trouble following directions. These recommendations will help children who have problems with directions become more successful regardless of the source. Follow this procedure:

C. Consider the context. If engrossed in some activity, your child may not even realize that you are speaking to him or her. If you do not get an immediate response, avoid the temptation simply to assume that your child is tuning you out. Consider waiting, or providing him or her with the courtesy of acknowledging that you are interrupting. Common courtesy is a big part of context analysis. Parents often get angry when they are interrupted. Some surveys of parents indicate that interrupting is the most aggravating thing their kids do regularly. Remember, courtesy cuts both ways. If you want to raise courteous children, treat your children with courtesy. Too often we forget that little children do have a world of their own. When we interrupt it to tell them to do something to satisfy a need of ours, they may feel annoyed by the intrusion. In the case of older children, who are in their room with the door closed, courtesy dictates that you knock and be given permission before entering. Please "knock" before entering your child's world. Whenever practical, do this by going to the area your child occupies and standing where your child can see you.

O. Observe yourself—take your TEMPERature. If you are not in the Action Zone, C.O.O.L. down as needed. Then, give the directions in a calm, reasonable way. Speak slowly and softly. Take a few moments to relax and regroup, if necessary. Be sure that you have eye contact with your child before you start giving directions. If needed, get down on his or her eye level. At a minimum, this insures that you have given your child every opportunity to pay attention to what you are saying.

O. Organize your options. Give the child *one* direction at a time. Children who have difficulty following directions commonly forget what you have told them if more than one instruction is given. Have the child repeat the instruction back to you. That way, you are sure the instruction has made it into the child's short-term memory. This step also gives you the opportunity to correct any misunderstanding the child might have about what it is that you want him or her to do.

L. Look to the future, ever mindful of the past. Imagery that allows you to visualize yourself staying C.O.O.L. and seeing your children follow through can be helpful. Use it as you approach them.

Other points to keep in mind that will help your children heed your instructions include the following:

Specify a time limit in which to complete the task and tell your child what it is. For example, if you ask the child to pick up his or her room, allow one to fifteen minutes, depending on the condition of the room.

Follow up by checking to see that the task has been completed within the allotted time. Setting a kitchen timer can remind both you and the child that you mean business, and that you will be following through. When you set the timer, you can also have a reminder to praise the child for doing the right thing in a timely manner.

Use the sandwich technique whenever possible. This is how it works. First, get the child's attention by reminding him or her of something done right, such as how nice the child's room looked after he or she cleaned it on Tuesday. Then tell the child the things to be done now. Lastly, praise the child for listening so attentively. Be sure to praise the positive things your child does. Distractible children need immediate feedback. The teaching process requires many repetitions and much follow-up.

When your goal is to help a child learn to follow instructions, use very few words. Be sure the child understands the words you have used. Follow up immediately. Avoid scolding, because it gives negative attention. Children can actually become addicted to negative attention. Your anger may even excite them. The excitement results in punishment later if they get overstimulated and forget part of the message. You know how impulsive and disorganized they can become when they get excited. Excitement is the last thing a distractible child needs when he or she is trying to concentrate on directions. It is very important that you stay calm, especially when you are dealing with a child who is struggling with a mental task such as schoolwork. We know that high physiological arousal levels that accompany stress are rooted in the fight or flight response. They seriously interfere with a person's ability to solve complex problems. The multiplication tables may not be too complex to you, but try telling that to a child who is struggling to learn them. Calmness is important to help your child understand instructions that affect other aspects of his or her life as well.

Clothes, Clean and Dirty!

Technique #1: For the occasional need to assist the younger child, try this:

First, be sure you have a clothes hamper.

Second, ask your child to put his or her dirty clothes in the hamper.

Third, after the first request, remind the child only once.

Fourth, if the child objects, ignores you, or throws a temper tantrum, take him or her by the arm, using only as much effort as necessary, and guide the child to the clothes. Be very positive. If the child goes limp, carry him or her.

Fifth, pick up the clothes with the child, guiding the child's hands until each garment has been placed in the hamper.

Technique #2: If messy clothes are a long-term problem:

First, purge the drawers and closets of old clothes, and keep only a seven-day supply within your child's reach.

Second, each night help select and lay out clothes for the morning. That way, you'll be ahead of the game.

If your child objects and says, "I can get myself ready!" Great! Give the child a chance. Say, "All right. I know you're getting older. So how about this? On days when you're dressed, groomed, and ready for breakfast on time, you handle your own clothes. But if you're not ready on time, I'll go back to laying out your clothes."

Remember, we're teaching independence! So give your child a chance, and praise your child when he or she gets it right!

Back up your rule with total consistency at this point. When your child does not keep his or her end of the bargain, go immediately back to the original rule. No nagging or scolding. Actions speak louder than words. Lay out his clothes that night.

Tomorrow is a new day and a new opportunity for your child to prove he or she can "do it myself."

Technique #3: Especially for older children:

First, make sure your older child knows where the clothes hamper is located. I know the child is familiar with the hamper's location. But pointing it out takes only seconds and sends a clear message that you expect compliance, not excuses.

Second, tell the child to use it.

Third, wash only the clothes that make it into the hamper.

Taking care of "floor laundry"—that's what we call the laundry that ends up on the floor rather than in the hamper—is your child's job. He or she will have to do it on Saturday morning, Friday afternoon, or at whatever time is convenient for you. Schedule the laundry session for a time when you're up to supervising laundry detail or brave enough to turn your child loose alone.

And then there's always . . .

The Parent's Pawn Shop

Having to pawn the video games, the stereo, CDs, the keys to the car, sports equipment, or other valuables can help a child learn the value of personal organization.

It works like this: If your child is unwilling to comply with reasonable demands for neatness, and the mess is driving you crazy, you clean it, for a price! If you charge $10 to do Nathan's room, and he's broke, the video game goes in the pawnshop until he buys it back. He can earn money by doing some chores you designate, like washing your car, or save enough out of allowances to get it out of hock. If the game is not out of hock within a reasonable amount of time — it's yours.

Toy Rotation

You say, "Toys are a mess!" Try this: Get some storage boxes or large plastic garbage bags, depending on how many toys there are. Pack up all but half a dozen favorite toys and put them away.

About once a month, rotate the toys. Take out one batch and bring in another. Rotation works well with preschool children. This may be helpful with children of elementary-school age as well. They earn the right to have two toy groups by keeping their room organized. If they backslide, and of course they probably will, go back to a single toy group.

How long they're limited to one toy group should depend on how well they conform. If they pick up their room on schedule for several weeks, you may choose to allow them two or more toy groups at a time.

On the other hand, if it's been a long, bitter struggle to get even one group of toys organized, wait until good organizational habits have been demonstrated for several weeks before allowing two groups.

Here's another technique:

The Sunday Box

Have a place for everything. At night, just prior to bedtime, have Jamal put his toys away. If he refuses, you pick them up—and put them in the Sunday box! This can be any lockable box. The trunk of your car might work just fine. Wherever it's located, this box is opened only on Sunday. Sunday may not be practical for everyone. If Thursday is your lucky day, make it a Thursday Box instead!

Of course, you'll want to explain about the Sunday Box and how it works before you begin using it. If the messy room is an extremely bad problem, you might introduce the idea in stages. For example, launch the program on Friday, then you open the box on Saturday, only one day later. That way, you're putting out a strong message: "This is a serious issue and I'm doing something about it!" But you are still allowing the child a little time to get used to the change.

Remember, to be effective and fair with any behavior program, consider how the rest of the family behaves as well. If your child lives in "Slobovia," don't expect him or her to become the only neat person in the household. You might even use the Sunday Box for Dad's socks, or Mom's shoes, or sister's dolls. That way Jamal isn't made to feel as if he alone is being punished for something that others in the family may be guilty of.

Designate a "Chore Hour"

Family cleaning day seems to have gone the way of the black-and-white TV, but what about designating, say, 9 to 10 A.M. Saturday as "Chore Hour." Be sure to inspect your child's work quality *before* cartoons are turned on. If the room is clean and inspected on Friday evening, of course, cartoons can be turned on earlier. You'll be surprised how clean a messy room can get! For extreme cases of "slo-bitis," room inspection may have to be a nightly ritual that takes place before the TV is turned on. Set a specific time for such cleanup. Remember, you must inspect. Set a slightly less rigid policy if you're not so well organized.

Exchange a Clean Room for TV Privileges

Here's how the well-organized approach might work. If the TV usually gets turned on between 3:00 and 3:30, set room inspection time at 2:50. Reinspect at 3:00. If the room passes, the TV is turned on. If it fails, no TV for thirty minutes. Then, if it is clean when the thirty minutes are up, turn on the TV. If your announcement of the "Clean Room for TV Privileges" is greeted by a temper tantrum, follow the tantrum reduction procedure.

The general, or less rigid, policy operates much like the policy I've just described, but it allows for greater flexibility. This might be more suitable for parents whose work schedules make it impossible for them to inspect at specific, timed intervals every day. You simply announce, with as much notice as is fair to the child, that there will be an inspection at such-and-such a time. Then go ahead as described. Don't be too surprised if, after a while, you're asked spontaneously to make an inspection. Reward such initiative. Be generous with praise and bonuses when the room is up to par.

Here's another messy room approach that develops initiative. Before the TV is turned on or some other reinforcer is made available, for example his bike or skateboard, Malcolm finds you and asks you to inspect his room or check his homework. If he passes, the bike is his for thirty minutes. If he flunks, he has ten minutes to get it right before you reinspect.

Homework: Check Early and Often.

Too often, homework time is a problem time. To keep your C.O.O.L. at the homework hour, check your child's work after five minutes. If help is needed, give it then. If your child seems to be doing well, check back in ten minutes. Avoid long periods of unassisted homework time until your child has demonstrated a consistent pattern of accurate work completed in a timely fashion.

CHAPTER 16

The Lying Game

Lies, deceptions, and distortions of the truth are maddening to parents. Preschoolers frequently make statements that are untrue, but they are not lying. Preschoolers don't have the ability to reliably distinguish fact from fantasy. As long as he or she believes in Santa and the Easter Bunny, we must question a child's ability to distinguish fact from fiction. A lie requires a decision to deceive. Children of preschool age never lie. Older children? Now that's a horse of a different color. Does this story sound familiar?

Father to ten-year-old Ben: "What grade did you get on the English test, son?" Ben's reply: "Oh! She didn't give the test back yet, Dad." While walking the dog that evening, Dad finds the English test near the curb. Guess what grade Ben made on the English test?

When was the last time your little Ben lied about his school grades? Ask yourself honestly. Did that lie raise your TEMPERature? If not, how about this scenario? Mom is cooking dinner when screams are heard from the family room. Mom: "Ben, did you hit Sissy?" Ben: "No, Mom, I don't know why she's crying!" Is this enough to make your hair turn gray? No doubt about it, children's lies can be a real aggravation.

Children usually lie to avoid pain. The pain may come from a belt, fear, shame, or even guilt. Lying to avoid a spanking is easy to understand. I daresay, many of us have done that a time or two ourselves. Fear itself is such an unpleasant emotion that adults spend millions of dollars each year on tranquilizers and therapists' bills to reduce the feeling of fear. Doesn't it seem reasonable that a child would lie to avoid the experience of fear? Shame is another form of pain. Children and adults don't want to experience pain, so they lie. Disapproval is another aversive experience that may encourage lying. If the child doesn't tell about the transgression, he or she doesn't risk disapproval from Mom or Dad. Still, it's hard for parents to understand why. "Why does he lie? I have told him so many times not to." Immediacy. Remember the principle of immediacy. It's not how big a reward or punishment is, it's the immediacy of the reward or punishment that will strengthen the behavior. That principle of immediacy has a lot to do with why kids keep on lying.

Let's consider what happens when a youngster is caught in a lie. Once he or she is caught, the child is afraid. Until he or she got caught, the child may have been worried or may have been blissfully naive. Believing he or she would not get caught, the child may even have forgotten what had been done and moved on to something else. Remember, your child is distractible and has a short attention span. Once he or she is caught—once you've got the goods on the child—fear starts. Fear is very unpleasant, correct? What is the most expeditious way of removing that unpleasant feeling of fear? Eliminate the problem! If the problem is a bad English paper, make the paper vanish. "I didn't have a bad English paper!" There goes the problem. There goes the fear. Ben believes that Dad won't see through the story. Pain is postponed. "Maybe Dad will forget about it by report card time." "Maybe I can get a better grade on a retest." "Maybe Mrs. Brown will feel sorry for me and give me a passing grade."

Ben is comfortable again. Comfortable, that is, until Mom and Dad find the paper and ask him about it. Once again, fear and anxiety get very strong. He may even feel the discomfort of guilt. But if that pain is less than the anticipated pain of resulting punishment or disapproval, he will not fess up. Remember, the principle of immediacy rules. Lying behavior is frequently maintained by immediate reduction of an unpleasant emotion. "But I've told you a thousand times. Tell me the truth and you won't get spanked." Still, he does it. "It drives me crazy! Why won't he just tell me the truth? It would be so much simpler!" By now you know how to answer the why question. Simply consult your crystal ball, right?—No way! Trying to learn why your children lie may actually increase lying. The interrogation to discover why is a form of negative attention. The interrogation may help blow off some adult steam, but it's hard to interrogate in a nonjudgmental way. So you are getting angrier with each question, right? Your nonverbal behavior, body language, and so on, is what your children are reading. The message is clear: "Mom is mad. I'm in for it now!"

Let's replay that scene as a C.O.O.L. parent.

Dad: "How did you do on the English test today, son?"

Son: "Mrs. Brown didn't give the test back yet, Dad."

Later, while walking the dog, Dad finds the paper. He begins to heat up, but then remembers the most effective thing he can do is to C.O.O.L. down. So he C.O.O.L.s down.

Dad

1. Considers the context triggers and consequences.
2. Objectively observes himself. Takes a few deep breaths. Scans his body for tension and relaxes his jaw. Where do you get tense? List your frequent tension traps below.

_____

_____

_____

Recalling one of his Forgettable Flare-ups reminds Dad to tell himself that "Ben has been trying to improve his grades. I'll give him a chance to tell his side of the story."

3. Organizes his options. Dad walks around the block—again. As he is walking, he scans his mind for angry self-talk that could accelerate his anger. List your most common thoughts and feelings when your child lies. Dad pictures a stop sign in his head and stops his angry thoughts.

_____

_____

_____

4. Looks to the future while learning from the past and living in the present. He recalls one of his Success Stories. It helps him to picture himself having a productive talk with Ben.

Dad substitutes a pleasant or neutral thought for the angry ones. For a moment Dad remembers the first fish Ben caught, the wildflowers Ben picked for Mom yesterday. Fill in the neutral or pleasant thoughts you can use to detoxify your anger.

_____

_____

_____

Lastly, Dad then asks himself some questions about his present state of mind: What kind of mood am I in tonight? Have I been drinking? Am I angry at anything other than Ben? When I was ten years old, how would I have handled a flunked test? Am I in the right frame of mind to help Ben? Will my reaction to this lie encourage Ben to rebel passively or to reflect on his actions and try harder to be truthful in the future?

What are some C.O.O.L. DOWN questions you need to ask yourself?

_____

_____

_____

Once he has C.O.O.L.ed down, Dad approaches his son:

Dad: "Son, I'm disappointed that you didn't tell me the truth about the test. Would you care to talk about it now?"

Son: Tells all!

Father: "I'm glad you told me the truth, but the video game will be put up until you master these parts of speech. I'll help you, son."

Remember, no one, not even Ben, enjoys flunking an English test. Ben failed the test because he was incapable of passing. Why was he incapable of passing this particular test? There could be many reasons. Maybe he did not study. Perhaps he was distracted in class. He may have been poorly taught. His knowledge could have been improperly measured. Many annoying kids have specific learning disabilities and are unfairly treated in a traditional classroom. Their knowledge is unfairly measured by traditional testing methods. Even the federal government has recognized the right of learning disabled students to have appropriate schooling. Parents would be better advised to help their children achieve rather than to punish them twice. Remember, Ben threw away the test paper because it was painful. How often would Ben throw away a candy bar?

Pain may come from the sting of the belt or the sting of the word. Fear, shame, or even guilt produce a lot of pain for kids. Difficult kids get punished so often they accumulate pain. Punishment can be a very effective way to stop undesirable behavior, but too much emotional pain, such as shame, guilt, and fear, can distort a child's self-image. Punishment should never involve shame. Children enter this world believing they are the center of the universe. The world revolves around them. In a typical family each new arrival is the subject of great anticipation. Each new baby is greeted with joy and celebration.

How can a child not feel he or she's the center of Mother's world? Adults comfort, coddle, and cuddle the normally active baby. He or she hears only words of love, sees only looks of love. As the child grows older, he or she is occasionally chastised for wrongdoing, and soon learns to do the right thing.

Contrast this typical situation with the early years of a hyperactive child. For months he or she is bumped around in Mother's womb. At times the child probably kept Mother awake at night. He or she may have even awakened Dad during the last few months. Finally the big day arrives, the day you both have waited almost a year for. Let the celebration begin. "What did you say, Grandmother? I can't hear you over the screams of the baby." "Mom, I wonder if he's got colic. He seems so fussy. Is he all right?"

"Sleep? What's that? This child doesn't seem to sleep. She even gets up at night. I found her in the yard riding her tricycle last night." "Take a nap? You must be kidding! Whitney hasn't napped since she was six months old." What began as a celebration of joy and love soon becomes a scene of concern, tension, frayed nerves, anger, and guilt. Quite a different self-concept for parent and child. No one likes hearing a baby cry. Crying may trigger anger rooted in fear, fatigue, or ignorance of what to do. Remember, the baby loves you. The baby's very life depends on you. The baby is *never* mad at you. Anger at an infant is extremely dangerous for the young child. A baby should *never* be shaken. Shaking a baby *one* time can cause brain damage, blindness, paralysis, retardation, even death. A baby's brain is loosely attached. His or her neck muscles are very weak. When a baby is shaken, the baby's brain crashes into the skull repeatedly. This can cause severe brain damage that cannot be seen. The damaged blood vessels also restrict blood to the cells in the brain. The cells then die. The baby is left with incurable brain damage. Be certain you are in the Action Zone *before* handling a baby. If you do shake a baby, take the baby to the hospital immediately and tell the doctor. Infants and toddlers should *never* be hit. When you are angry at an infant, take your TEMPERature immediately. If you are out of the Action Zone, put the baby in a safe place as you C.O.O.L. down. If this doesn't work, call a friend or Parents Anonymous. They have a twenty-four-hour free parents helpline.

A Walkman or similar device can help you keep your C.O.O.L. or prepare you to check your child. When the child's cry is fussy, the Walkman can be used to review C.O.O.L. skills or play comforting music. This handy electronic gadget can be your best friend in times of trouble. Depending on your need and mood, you can use it to play relaxing music, review instructions for proper use of time-out, or to lighten up a tense situation with some humorous anecdotes. The uses are limited only by your own ingenuity. Certain uses are especially recommended.

When you are down on yourself, play your affirmations and self-valuing messages. Make a list of ten things you value about yourself. If they bring a smile, so much the better. Dictate the ten good points about you onto the tape. Now make a list of ten things you love and value about your challenging child. Dictate them as well. Sometimes music will inspire peace, calm, and love. Use it.

Nourish your happy memories. We parents are often so overwhelmed by the demands placed on us, we forget to smell the roses.

Happy Memory Journal

Plan to recreate some roses with a Happy Memory Journal and Scrapbook. When you are in an especially good mood, make a few notes about the happy experience that helped your mood. Include a photo or souvenir in your Happy Memory Journal. Souvenirs might include:

1. 1/2 oz. of sand from the beach
2. A leaf from the meadow
3. A movie ticket stub
4. A receipt from a meal
5. _____

Make a record. Create your family's Funniest Home Audios or Videos. Use your happy notes and souvenirs to help you recreate happy memories.

Get the kids involved. Kids love to record their ideas on tape. As a psychotherapist, I learned long ago that young children who may be reluctant to discuss problems love to tell their troubles to the tape recorder. They also absolutely adore putting happy tales on tape. This can be a fun activity that will play handsome dividends in chasing the blues and helping you regain your optimism in times of need.

Make it easy on yourself. Don't attempt this taping immediately after the happy time. The children may be overstimulated or tired. Make the happy tape when your child is rested, contented, happy, and cooperative. Most children have trouble taking turns, so plan to record the kids alone. Tell young children that you're making a happy tape to remind yourselves of how much you enjoyed your trip to the library story hour. Ask the child to record what he or she liked best about the experience. Tell the child that this tape is for Mom and Dad. The child will also get to make his or hers. You choose the length and reserve the right to edit. Limit each message. A minute may be long enough. No more than three minutes. For your personal pick-me-ups, use your creativity, but don't feel obligated. No matter what, remember, "This tape is for you!"

The kids will also love separately recording their own happy messages. Limit the happy messages to three minutes for starters. You and/or your spouse may record a brief happy recollection on the child's tape. Include your reflection or memory for each child separately—no longer than one minute per child. Sometimes thirty seconds will be plenty. If the child likes your message, fine. If he or she seems to object—they almost never do—cut it short. Be sure to include at least one, but no more than three, happy emotions that accompany your memory. Children love to listen to themselves, so let them listen to happy memories on nights they are hard to get to bed or asleep. The children's tapes will help them to relax with a happy message at bedtime. In times of stress and confusion, the happy tapes will stimulate comforting, soothing memories of love, security, and good times. Remember, children love sameness, consistency, and familiarity. The happy tapes ensure a comforting presence that will give Mom and Dad a break as well. Tapes are inexpensive and easily modified. Interviews with grandparents, favorite aunts and uncles, and special soothing friends can be added to the collections. When expanding the tape collection, be sure to avoid overstimulating messages. Messages must be positive and upbeat, but do *not* make them exciting.

ALL MESSAGES SHOULD BE POSITIVE. NO LECTURES!

Child-to-child messages are another use for the tape. If children are instructing themselves with what they should and shouldn't do in certain situations, they will be more likely to hear and heed than if subjected to an adult lecture.

Dedicate yourself to the practice of "catching them being good." And when they are, let them know you noticed. This is especially important with children whose behavior is so annoying that they have become accustomed to being corrected and disciplined almost constantly. This may be a little tricky at first because some kids get into so much trouble they become addicted to nagging—addicted to negativism.

For those addicted to negativism, the transfer to positive addiction may be slower. But it will occur. It's hard to imagine, but children can get so used to being criticized and yelled at that they seek out negative attention. As in the days of the Wild West, it is better to be wanted for murder than not to be wanted at all! Negative addiction is a "crazy maker" for parents and teachers alike. The frustration and anger you express is actually strengthening the undesirable behavior in your children. You can avoid negative addiction by catching kids being good.

TO CATCH THEM BEING GOOD, YOU MUST FIRST CATCH YOURSELF.

Plan ahead to catch the kids being good. First check your TEMPERature, and take appropriate steps to C.O.O.L. down if necessary. If things are really hectic, pick a time when your spouse or a friend is there to help.

Try this for an afternoon or evening:

Set the kitchen timer, or buy one of the new high-tech vibrating timers.

When the timer goes off, observe the kids. Find something positive to praise them for.

This sample schedule can help you to set your timer:

At 6:00 P.M. set the timer for ten minutes
At 6:10 P.M. set the timer for fifteen minutes
At 6:25 P.M. set the timer for ten minutes
At 6:35 P.M. set the timer for thirty minutes
At 7:05 P.M. set the timer for fifteen minutes
At 7:20 P.M. set the timer for thirty minutes
At 7:50 P.M. set the timer for ten minutes

Feel free to create your own schedule if this one seems too rigid. But please do set up a schedule. Follow it for at least one month. By planning to catch your children being good, you will break the negative attention cycle. You will enjoy your children more if you focus on the lovable things they do or try to do. Even if they are arguing, praise them for not hitting. "I know you were upset with Monica, Malcolm, but I'm proud of you because you used words instead of hands to let her know your were angry." Give your children hugs and kisses. Then leave the area till the timer goes off again. If they are locked in mortal combat, have Dad separate them. Tomorrow night Dad can be the "Good Guy" and mom can be the Bouncer!

Happy Board

Obtain a small bulletin board and place it on the door in the children's room or on the refrigerator. When you catch them being good, Praise-Hug-Kiss. Make a note and pin it to the Happy Board. Create a page of affirmations:

Thank you for playing cooperatively with:

_____

Thank you for listening politely to:

_____

Thank you for being sweet to:

_____

Shock and confusion can increase the power of your praise. If the children are used to you yelling when they are noisy, they may be in the habit of aggravating you and enjoying your exasperation. By focusing on the positive, you will shock and confuse them. This contrast with your typical response will make the positive more effective.

Compliance Training is a surefire solution to get you and your child working together in a positive way. Here's how it works:

1. Pick a time when both you and your child seem to be in a good mood. Be sure he's not engrossed in some distracting activity or a favorite TV program.
2. Plan three or four requests you can make that will be very easy for the child to obey, such as:

"Please hand me my glasses."
"Come here and give me a hug."
"Would you please hand me that magazine?"
"Can you carry this bowl to the table?"

Be sure to praise the child when he or she does what you've asked. Make sure your body language is warm and accepting. Smile and give your child a hug. Be sensitive to your child's mood. If your child is older, don't embarrass him or her by becoming too enthusiastic with your praise. Notice how your child responds and adjust your behavior accordingly. If your child seems embarrassed, tone it down. If he or she lights up, pour on the praise! Remember—a reinforcer is only a reinforcer if it increases the behavior that follows it. Our goal is to increase the desirable behavior. Plan to use compliance training twice a day for at least two weeks. You'll be certain to "catch them being good."

Be positive and give instructive praise, such as the following:

"It feels good when you do as I ask!"
"We have so much fun when you cooperate!"
"Look how happy the dog is to have that drink of cool water!"

Compliance Training is one form of insurance against negative addiction. By planning to be positive, you're building your family's emotional bank account. You might say that Compliance Training can help you save up good feelings for a rainy day. Don't be discouraged if you don't see a lot of positive changes right away. Most difficult children have gotten a great deal of negative attention, even if they're only three or four years old. This buildup of negative energy will take time, persistence, and planning to overcome. Think of Compliance Training as a lifestyle change, not a light switch. If you believe in it, use it consistently, and follow through, you will send a powerful signal to your child. It will be picked up because it is backed up.

CHAPTER 17

Rewards, Bribery, and Reinforcement

As a C.O.O.L. parent it's important for you to understand the difference between reward, bribery, and reinforcement. Many parents say they do not want to bribe their child in order to get correct behavior, and I agree. But a reward and a bribe are two very different things.

A bribe is something you offer in advance of desired behavior. "Here, darling. I'll let you eat your dessert first, but you have to promise to eat all your lovely peas and carrots, too!"

A reward is something that is given after the desirable action has been performed. Bounty hunters get rewards after bringing in bad guys, not before.

As a C.O.O.L. parent you'll be using an efficient method of developing good habits and behavior. It's called reinforcement. When used correctly and consistently, reinforcement encourages desirable behavior. Bribes, on the other hand, seldom work as reinforcers and are generally seen as manipulative. Reinforcement can only be judged by its effect on the behavior it follows. No increase in behavior—no reinforcement occurred. Simple, right?

This is a major difference between reinforcement, bribery, and reward.

It doesn't matter how big!
It doesn't even matter how expensive!
If it doesn't increase the behavior it follows—
It ain't reinforcement!

This concept is so important that I am going to dedicate this chapter to reinforcement.

Contingency Management

The most convenient way to use the reinforcement technique for developing desirable behavior is a method called Contingency Management. Here's how it works. Instead of resorting to a bribe, you establish a relationship based on something else happening first. For example, you might say, "You get to do what you want to do after you've done what you have to do." "You may play a video game after your homework is done." "Make your bed and clean your room before you go outside to play on Saturday morning."

There are two primary factors that affect the success of Contingency Management.

The first is immediacy. It is far more effective, for example, to say "You may play a video game after your homework is done," than to say, "If you have a B average on your report card next month, you'll get a new bicycle." Other strong immediate reinforcers would include allowing the child to watch TV, listen to music, or have telephone privileges as soon as his or her homework is completed.

Change Wish List

What are some habits you wish to change?

1. _____

2. _____

3. _____

Only three habits to change?

I know, you're probably thinking, this guy must be kidding. If I only had three habits to change, I wouldn't be reading this book!

Why such a short list? To change habits, you must start small to accomplish big things. Rome wasn't built in a day and neither were undesirable habits unlearned in a day. Pick the easiest habit to change first. Why? It's important that you and your child experience early successes. Remember, you are learning new skills, techniques, and attitudes. In the early stages of learning, a lot of reinforcement insures success, and success is reinforcement.

Another reason to think small—your patience may be strained already. Remember, that's why you bought this book. So be gentle on yourself. Why set yourself up for disappointment? As you become more skilled, you'll break down big goals into small steps. Then you will be better equipped to tackle the tough habits. After some initial success, you will have begun to improve your relationship with your child. He or she will start wanting to please you again. Kids don't enjoy being the bad guys in the family, but they are so annoying so much of the time they lose faith in their ability to be able to please you. What do you think happens then?

What's even worse, these children begin to see themselves as failures at pleasing adults—any adults. Conflicts with authority figures multiply and a negative self-image is developed. So when thinking habit change, Think Small—Accomplish Big!

The second critical factor in habit change is consistency. Especially in the early stages, consistency is critical. Establish the rule that good things are based on something else happening first. Apply it every time it is appropriate. When using contingency management to start desired behavior, particularly in younger children, use continuous reinforcement. When the behavior is established, make the reinforcement *less* predictable or *more* expensive. Doing so has been proven scientifically to strengthen behavior patterns once they are learned. You can do this by requiring slightly more work for the same amount of reinforcement. Give out reinforcement like smiles, praise, or hugs for behavior that is already well established. Think of this as preventative maintenance. To maintain good habits, contingency management is a natural. Simply stick with "You must do what you have to do before you get to do what you want to do." A reminder of the old notion of work before play is very effective for well-established habits. Another positive approach to maintaining good behavior is to talk about how proud you are of Casey's report card in front of people she wants to please. Favorite relatives, family friends, or that "old biddy down the street" who called to complain about Casey's irresponsibility when the dog got out and into her garbage.

If your child has started puberty and recoils from public praise around peers, don't give it. If praise produces unpleasant emotions, it can function as punishment instead of reinforcement.

There are some exceptions to this rule. If your child has been diagnosed with ADHD or, like Derrick, has problems with concentration and impulsivity caused by something else, you are better advised to be more rather than less consistent with the reinforcement schedule, until you are certain that the targeted behavior is very well learned. This is particularly true if your child is very distractible. Some children are so distractible that it can be difficult to establish the connection between behavior and consequence.

It is best that you learn to monitor the results that the consequences have on behavior. But I can assure you that it will be necessary to be creative in selecting and changing reinforcers. The best time to change is as soon as the reinforcer begins to lose effectiveness or just prior to that time. Again, in evaluating this situation, consider the context. The reinforcer may be losing effectiveness because you have reached the point of diminishing returns. When it comes to the effectiveness of most reinforcers, too much of a good thing is still too much.

Say Grandma is visiting. She insists on buying Derrick any treat he wants. Kathy has his allowance set up so that he is earning money for the treats and the arcade by doing chores. When Grandma takes him to the arcade, she gives Derrick three rolls of quarters every time. Guess what happens to the power of the reinforcer? Because he had his fill of the arcade, the arcade is *not* a reinforcer at this time. Reinforcers are *not* things. Like time-out, a reinforcer is defined by a relationship. A reinforcer isn't always something you say you want. It may not even be something your child says he or she wants. A reinforcer is only a reinforcer when it works. Like time-out, the criteria for a reinforcer is the relationship it has with the behavior. The reinforcer must influence behavior by increasing the behavior it follows. If it doesn't, it is not a positive reinforcer. Two starving people would fight over a crust of stale bread that would go unnoticed by them following a meal at Mom's All You Can Eat Buffet. The degree of want or deprivation has a lot to do with the power of a reinforcer to influence behavior. The more you want it, the more powerful it is. When it comes to reinforcers, absence truly does make the heart grow fonder.

It is important that Kathy learn about reinforcement for other reasons also. Do you recall our discussion of Stages of Change? You learned about the Precontemplation, Contemplation, Preparation, Action, Maintenance, and Termination stages of change. Remember that reinforcement for YOU is the key to motivating your long-term maintenance of C.O.O.L. habits. Hopefully, most of your reinforcement will occur naturally, but if you get in a situation that requires you to "tough it out," be sure to drop a quarter in your cookie jar for each C.O.O.L. thought you substitute for a hot trigger. Use your quarters to pay for a sitter, an ice cream sundae, or anything your heart desires. But be sure to do it often. After you make out your list of reinforcers for your children, do the same for yourself!

People are sometimes surprised to learn that after reinforcement techniques have been in use for some time, making the reward less predictable will actually strengthen the behavior. But it is true. Think about it. What is a strong habit anyway? It's a habit that is very resistant to change. Remember how hard it was to quit smoking? A strong habit is a persistent habit. One that persists when an immediate reward is not forthcoming. After the grandparents left, Kathy and Derrick struggled for several days. After Derrick went to the mall with no money in his pocket for the game room, his interest in the room miraculously returned. Once a habit is well established in the child, you can strengthen it by occasionally breaking your rule.

Mario is six and he had been making his bed every day for two weeks before going out to play. Today, Malcolm calls to invite Mario to go swimming with his family. They are leaving in ten minutes. Carla thinks to herself, "Would this be a good time to tell Mario, 'Go ahead, son, you've done so well, I'll make your bed this morning. But tomorrow it's right back to first making your bed then playing outside. OK?'" Yes is her answer. Mario's response is gratitude.

Mario: "Sure, Mom! Thanks." Tomorrow, it was business as usual. Carla had built goodwill with her son and strengthened Mario's self-talk, such as, "I can please Mom. Doing my job does have its rewards." Result: Mario will be more likely to want to please Carla in the future. Mario will be less likely to resent authority in the future. Carla will feel more affection for Mario in the future.

Plan B

Sometimes things don't go as planned. Monday morning comes and Mario rushes out to play, leaving his room a mess. Carla doesn't despair! She thinks, "He's only human. Behavior isn't 100 percent predictable, so I'll do the following."

1. Begin my C.O.O.L.-down procedure
2. Go and find Mario, *now*. *Quietly* but *firmly* bring him home. Have Mario clean his room. Excuse him, then let him return to play. Habit change will frequently run a zigzag course.

"OK, now that I know what he likes, how do I dole it out in an effective way?" There is no way to know the power of a reinforcer in advance. So you must experiment and observe the results! For items like a Saturday movie, Carla decides that Mario can earn the price of admission one day at a time. She is certain to spell out clearly what he must do to earn his way to the show.

How do you know which reinforcers will work with your child? Easy. Just observe. Identify those things that are high-priority activities for the child and use them as reinforcers.

Your child's favorite pastimes are a good place to start:

Activities _____

Things _____

Reactions from you!

Approval_____   Smiles_____   Hugs_____   Disapproval_____

Foods _____

Money _____

Friends _____

Games _____

Movies _____

TV _____

By now you get the picture. Once you've identified and are using the most appropriate reinforcers, don't forget to establish limits that are appropriate as well. For example, the child should be allowed to earn free play, TV, or video games in set blocks of time, say ten minutes, rather than just being allowed to go off and watch TV or play "until bedtime." Reinforcers do not have to be material "things" to be effective. In fact, the natural reinforcers such as a smile, sincere praise, a positive greeting, or a hug are really the most effective reinforcers of all in the long run. But tangible reinforcers are necessary for high-maintenance kids.

The ambition of self-starters or intrinsically motivated people comes from their ability to automatically and consciously anticipate successful outcomes for their efforts. Their history of success constructs these images. Reinforcement documents the success of their efforts. This information is very important in the early stages of learning what they can expect of themselves. This internalized expectation of success keeps them going when others would quit. Internalized images of self-efficacy spring from positive judgments of an ability to succeed. These images motivate self-starters to try harder. These people are sometimes said to be psychologically hardy. They do better in life because they are committed, determined to do well. Schoolwork, their jobs, and other activities are important to them. They also believe they have the power to influence their lives. Reinforcement for jobs well done contributes to this belief. This belief enables these people to accept responsibility for their actions. The combination of realistic visions of what they can do well, with the skills and talents that they have or foresee themselves developing, frees them from fear of failure. This freedom allows them to see life as a challenge. This mind-set fosters ambition and diffuses defensiveness.

Of course, you may also want to use an allowance and special activities as reinforcers. As success builds, you will help your child internalize the ambition created by reinforcement by pairing it with constructive, informative feedback. This can be customized depending on your particular situation. It works well in helping teach decision- and choice-making skills to your child. Reinforcement is a very powerful tool, but everyone has a comfort zone. Beware of pushing too hard for perfection.

Pushing people for perfection opens many doors to anger. I can't tell you how many times after the initial, major problems have been taken care of, parents will start revealing some of their perfectionist fantasies about their children's initiative and responsibilities.

"I don't know why Jamal just doesn't take the trash out without being asked." "I wish just once Megan would clean up the messes she makes in her room without being told." Anger problems of at least two types result from unrealistically high expectations of people, while mutual anger and a sense of futility destroy positive motivation. That leads to the nothing-to-lose logic—or should I say illogic—that is a major anger escalator. Children naturally want to please their parents. When children begin to think that it will be impossible to do so, they experience a major sense of disillusionment. Their behind stings pretty regularly from the spankings they get and their heart hurts from the harsh words that their imperfections produce. The result is a nothing-to-lose logic.

Casey was a prime example. Abandoned by her biological father, who had abused and neglected her, she and her mother Laura set out to make a new life for themselves. Mom married a man who fathered three more children. While the new family, grandparents and all, doted on the younger children, Daddy number two dominated and eventually molested Casey. Mom felt so guilty that she pulled away from Casey even more. She was simply unable to deal with her guilt. Truth be known, she was pretty angry at Casey. Now that Protective Services was involved, Donald had to move out.

Since Casey was the oldest of the four children, Laura insisted that Casey pick up the slack that was left after Donald was forced out of the home. Casey was only eight, but she felt like eighty. All that responsibility. It seemed that nothing she did was good enough. The lack of positive reinforcement in her life caused her to become increasingly disillusioned. This disillusionment at her inability to please her mom made her very angry at her mother. She began to think of herself as a three-time loser. Her real father didn't want anything to do with her, her adopted father molested her, and now she couldn't please her mother. Casey was one angry child. Her anger was easier to feel than the shame of rejection and fear of abandonment it masked. Somebody was going to share her pain. One way to get mother's attention was to mistreat the little ones.

Since Mom was the closest and most recent to break her heart, Mom was going to be one perfectionist who knew what it felt like to fail. Disappointing a perfectionistic parent is a surefire way to get that parent's goat.

Older kids have many different ways to punish parents. Babies and normal children younger than seven or so don't know better. I think most of the more adventurous kids, the ones who get more than their share of punishment, have played the "get back" game more than once on their journey to autonomy. Sometimes the extremes of a child's hostile behavior to a parent can cause the child to feel guilt, shame, and other healthy emotions that teach the child's impulsive self a lesson.

I have been doing therapy with children, teens, and adults since 1968. I can't tell you how many times I have started laying the ground rules for marital, family, or group psychotherapy with a discussion of what the clients expect from me and what I expect from them in order to develop an effective working relationship. I always make it a point to require each family member to agree to "not punish another" for what they hear or don't hear in the psychotherapy session that either offends or otherwise hurts them. Obviously, the goal of psychotherapy is to learn more constructive ways to handle feelings, but the journey can be an arduous one. The comment about punishing typically elicits a few chuckles, but rarely have I had a high-maintenance child or adolescent deny or refute my contention that kids punish parents in a variety of ways. They can do this, for example, by behaving worse than they would usually behave following a session in which they were displeased. Punishment of parents is simply a childish manipulative ploy. The terms we often use to describe impulsive, self-centered, self-destructive, or hostile actions include "childish," "immature," originating from the "child within."

Children punish parents by doing things that scare, worry, intimidate, embarrass, or reject them. This pattern of manipulation is learned in the home, from media and peers. Children tend to become like or to identify with aggressors. If you use excessive amounts of physical or emotional punishment, your children learn to be more aggressive. There is a wealth of research as well as common-sense information that documents the fact that people who observe that aggression or crime pays are more likely to behave aggressively than those who see the opposite. It's a kind of "Monkey see, Monkey do" situation when it comes to aggressive behavior. This type of anger accelerator is very much a part of unhealthy parent-child interactions. So if you don't want butter, don't churn.

Admittedly, Casey's situation was quite extreme, but frankly not all that uncommon. The principle that positive reinforcement is necessary to build positive relationships and self-esteem is among the most widely accepted in all of behavioral science. Casey proved the point, at an unfortunately high emotional cost, that perfectionism doesn't pay. The Time Machine can help you review the appropriateness of your expectations. Use it to reacquaint yourself with the perceptions of task difficulty and the ability to do a good job that you experienced at a similar age.

Reconnecting with your past will help you to understand your child's emotional needs, styles of thinking, and desires for approval. This will help you to be more of a positive reinforcer for your child. Other things you can do to prevent perfectionism from ruining your relationship include talking to friends and family, and even asking your children for feedback. Parenting classes and support groups can also help you to set your sights appropriately. This will also help insure that you dispense more positive reinforcement. When you do so, your children's behavior will be more predictable and you will experience more feelings of success and confidence in your role as a parent.

CHAPTER 18

The Art of Compromise

Do they fuss, fume, and fight continually? Is your family more like the Hatfields and McCoys than you would like them to be? The tools of compromise can change all that. The use of a Family Forum will help you implement and reinforce the tools of change. This is a time you set aside to listen and talk to each other. No TV, no CD—just you and your family. Use of the Forum at least once a week will definitely reduce the fussing and fighting in your family.

Start by learning the difference between healthy conflict and abusive conflict. In a healthy family, you will find competition, jealousy, anger, and power struggles. In healthy families, divisive feelings, values, and beliefs are aired within an atmosphere of love and mutual respect. Respect for authority and order is combined with an openness to new ideas. Healthy families fight, but they fight fair. Differences of opinion or priorities are seen as opportunities for problem solving, not bloodletting. Healthy strife is solution oriented. Attitude is the first tool. "In your face" confrontation is out; win/win collaboration is in. We have a problem, so we will try to find a solution, or agree to disagree—these thoughts guide healthy disagreement.

Disagreement, of course, may have a price if the choice to disagree proceeds to violating family rules.

In the dysfunctional family, confrontation and competition become an end in themselves. Power struggles and jealousies take on a life of their own. Winning at any cost is the rule. The fact that winning at any cost wounds the hearts and minds of those you love doesn't seem important in the dysfunctional family.

Of course, discipline and consequences may come out of a Family Forum. But the purpose of the Forum is not to sit the children down for the magic lecture that will set them straight once and for all. The meeting is designed to teach your family how to develop a problem-solving style.

The second tool of compromise is clarity. Family aggression often results from ignorance or fear of change. Ignorance of the range of feelings that exist, their importance, sometimes even their presence, is common. This situation contributes enormously to the emotional gridlock that causes so much family frustration. One of the main reasons angry people don't discuss their emotions is that they don't know what words to use. Developing the ability to name emotional needs and feelings should be a top priority in such instances. Most of us only learn the names of a handful of feelings. One of the first things I inquire about when someone is having temper trouble is that person's ability to name emotions. Deceptively simple, but devastating if you can't do it. One can hardly be expected to discuss constructive methods of meeting emotional needs if they can't even be named. How many emotions can you name? How about the persons you argue with or get angry at most often? What grade would they get on a test of their ability to name and define fifty common feelings?

Consistency is tool number three. Your body language should be consistent with your words. Negotiations may be conducted using "sign language," but that can be very imprecise. Are your physical signs saying stop, while your words say go? Giving feedback on consistency between signs and words people use when they are angry is a big part of my job when I do family therapy.

The fourth tool for successful compromise is courtesy. Courtesy always improves the outcome. The golden rule of compromise is "speak unto others as you would have them speak unto you."

Courage is the fifth tool. Too often we hold our tongues because we are fearful of offending or hurting another's feelings. C.O.O.L. skills can help you hold down emotional arousal and say what needs to be said to the person who should hear it. Courtesy and an adequate vocabulary will help you say it directly and tactfully.

Credibility is tool number six. It comes from consistency between talk and action. Consistency builds credibility quicker than anything. If you say what you mean and act accordingly, you will soon become credible.

Commitment is tool number seven. Studies of people who change crippling habits have proved definitively that commitment will eventually win out. We also know that psychologically hardy people are committed to something important to them. High achievers in sports or any field of endeavor are extremely committed. Chronically depressed people who are helped by psychotherapy often report that the commitment of their therapist is what helped them the most. Chronic depression, anxiety, and anger problems are often maintained by "learned helplessness." The belief that you are powerless to change has devastating consequences. In contrast, happy people report that they have high levels of control and commitment. Commitment to work with communication and C.O.O.L. skills will give you the best possible chance of achieving success in the long run.

A key to opening the doors to healthy problem solving is recognizing the shades of emotion and self-talk that trigger angry explosions. Reinforce yourself for using triggers for happy, optimistic self-talk that emphasizes your options for mastery and harmony.

All-or-none thinking too often creates passions that polarize family members into armed camps of extremists. So jealously do they guard their emotional turf, you might think that their very life depended on winning someone over to their point of view. Anger can distort your perceptions to such an extent that you become blind to other points of view, often to an extent that would be impossible if you allowed yourself to feel love or compassion instead of anger. When we are angry, we frequently say "I'm mad." Remember the definition of *mad* in the Introduction? Mad behavior lacks the balance of normal reality checks. I guess that's why we call it madness. It allows you to feel justified in treating loved ones harshly. At times of high hostility, expressing differences of opinion or conflicting needs and notions can actually become dangerous. When it comes to family, we are talking forever. Please choose your "hills to die on" very carefully.

Tony has made a huge turnaround in that regard. In the following excerpt from a C.O.O.L. parent therapy group, Tony and other parents—including some of the ones whose names came up earlier in the book—provide us with insights based on their experiences and personal reflections. "I've noticed that we seem to have three different kinds of meetings at our house. One, I guess, you'd call planning powwows. They include talking about everyday events. Touching base, if you will. Of course, there are still nonnegotiables, but the statement of what is and isn't negotiable comes only when I am in the Action Zone, and only after a trip in the Time Machine. If it's a moral issue we are discussing, I consult with my pastor before taking a hard-line position. I also study what Scripture has to say on the subject from several vantage points. I invite the kids to do the same. We also have the problem-solving sessions. Topics like who is responsible for what chores, where can we find more time, what kind of schedule should we put together for the holiday break, are common. Other examples might include who gets the video game first, or how do we improve school grades? You know, that kind of stuff. Crisis councils are the most provocative but they help a lot to defuse anger and focus our energies on solutions to problems. Yeah," said Tony, "we have had a few of those at our house. Like when Carl and Barry got the moonlight madness, sneaking out in the middle of the night, taking the car, who knows what else. The time Officer Robinson called our house. That was a serious crisis.

"We find that the context of the meetings creates different types of attitudes. At the powwow, we are all really laid back. Anything goes at those discussions. When problem solving, we're more focused. We have to pay a lot more attention to our anger levels. I tend to get touchy quick. During the crisis councils, there is a lot of PATing ourselves, taking breaks, and backing off. We've come up with some of the guidelines that have been most helpful at our home. Maybe they'll be useful at yours.

"Some of the guidelines that seem to work best for us are these. Remember to use 'I' statements. In other words, when I am irritated with the kids, the first thing I found that helps is to 'own' my irritation. I do this by labeling it. I tell them, 'I feel angry.' Instead of saying, 'You make me mad.' They seem to take it better when I don't start by blaming them for my feelings.

"The next thing I do is ask, 'What makes you think the way you do?' I try to help them to clarify the beliefs and needs or sometimes wants that are directing their train of thought. Often, that's all it takes for the light to come on and the storm is over. If Carl has triggered my anger, I might ask, 'Are you trying to make me mad?' He almost always says no and then goes on to tell me what he is really thinking."

Danielle finds that if she uses the "I" statement to let her children know how she is feeling and *then* tells them what she would *prefer* they do the next time, she gets better results.

"Danny used to be like Carl," added Todd. "He answers more now that I ask more often. There really is something to this communication stuff. It has certainly helped me keep my cool."

"I'm pretty intuitive," Danielle observed. "I find that most of the time I know what my kids are going to do."

"Yes," said Todd, "but what about that other 30 percent? That can be disaster. I don't know about you but I have to admit that the mind-reading routine really aggravates Danny. That's why I ask clarifying questions. I am not good at mind reading. Most of the time the kids his age are fighting for respect anyway. How many times have you hassled over, 'You're treating me like a little kid.' To my way of thinking, I am just giving him a face-saving way to think through the problem from another point of view. It helps our meetings go smoother. One of the things we find particularly helpful is to be sure everyone knows that they can take a time-out, call a truce if they need to. The last thing I want is for all of us to get so heated up that we wind up angry and fighting instead of problem solving.

"Our Family Forums, particularly the problem solving ones, are just that. Problem-solving sessions. Nobody is allowed to get off by pulling power plays and simply attacking someone else. That goes for Danielle and me as well as the kids."

"I noticed, when the crisis came, when I got that 3 A.M. call, I was really steamed," Tony observed. "I had to use every C.O.O.L. skill in the book. But it worked. I waited to talk to Carl until I was more rested. I tried to put myself back in time to get an idea of what could have possibly been going through his mind. I even checked it out by asking clarifying questions. I deliberately tried to avoid the bazooka blasts. I know that the Family Forum has helped me to keep my cool. I get to know more of what's going on. Frankly, I plan to use the meetings to practice my C.O.O.L. skills. Throughout the meetings I make sure that I ask clarifying questions. I try to avoid backing him into corners. We have found that we take fewer extreme points of view. I am making a concerted effort to listen more and lay off the blaming and accusations. I ask for lots of input. I guess you could say that I am trying to remember that I am the adult. This is not a level playing field. I'm operating from the power position when I relate to my son. I try to recall a quotation I read somewhere that stuck in my head. 'Proof of virtue is to possess boundless power without abusing it.' We all want to feel like winners. I'm here to create a climate of understanding. I do it by finding out what emotional needs my kids have that I may not be aware of. That encourages acceptance of beliefs I know are right, not rebellion. Sure, I still play the heavy when necessary. I just don't find myself in that position so often anymore.

"Letter writing is a tool that is helpful when we have problems to solve. We turn it around a little bit in the problem-solving session. Each member of the family writes a letter to a stranger about the family member he or she is having a problem with. Three minutes are allowed for writing and three minutes response time to make their points verbally. In the letter they must identify the parent or sibling's good points as well as the bad points. It's a take off on the Thinking Zone idea that we use when Derrick or Camille has done something we disapprove of. It helps us to see what they need at this point in their lives and what is important to them. It also helps to let them know what is important to us. Stressors and pressures we have been under lately often get aired as well."

Larry and Kathy make it a point to have their meetings whether the family is in crisis or everything is going great. Close, intimate relationships usually require time together. I know this isn't always true. I have friends from childhood who live a thousand miles away. When we get on the phone, it seems like just yesterday. Often it has been years since we've spoken. That's different. The need for time together has a lot to do with how your time and energy use is perceived by the family. If they believe that you are gone because of an extremely solid reason, they can accept it better. Like providing basic food and shelter, for example. They might not resent you as much as they do when you appear to have all the necessities and keep working for more. When you are driven by strong achievement needs, your perception of what's necessary and what isn't will probably be quite different from that of your child. Their strongest need at that time may be to feel valued, significant, or important in your eyes. They might resent your absence more for this reason. The resentment may be suppressed, but no one enjoys being ignored by those who claim to love them the most.

Human attention, interest, and affection are among the most powerful influences on behavior that I know of. Please try to give them for behavior and attitudes that you want to see repeated and to withhold them from those that you would rather live without. Use your power wisely. The Family Forum is a great way to demonstrate support for communication, negotiation, and compromise.

Meeting time can also include a family game. This works well when no one has an issue to consider. Relationship games will make it easier to keep your date for the Family Forum when the living is easy. There are three or four games we have found that have been very useful in this regard. They can be purchased from several mail order catalogs. The Self-esteem Game has been around for quite some time. It is a great little game. It's fun to play, the kids have as much chance of winning as adults do, and it will get you talking about feelings in a way that the kids don't seem to mind at all. In fact, they look forward to playing this game. There is also another one that they enjoy called Stop, Relax, and Think. This one helps to reinforce some of the C.O.O.L. skills such as belly breathing, muscle scanning and relaxing, and positive self-talk. Children like the fact that there are activities throughout the game that require everyone to get up and move around. It's good practice and good fun. Never Say Never is one I use quite often in my practice. It is a very inspirational game. The kids love it. They read about people who become famous despite learning or physical handicaps. People like Tom Cruise and Cher, for example, who became movie stars despite dyslexia.

The kids enjoy playing the Ungame. It has been around for some time. It is a noncompetitive game. No one wins, no one loses. I used to consider it rather pointless but the kids seem to love it. Card games are also a big favorite. One deck in particular has cards with suits of feelings instead of the usual. Kids get to express their feelings on any issue they choose. A feeling version of Go Fish or Rummy can be lots of fun. The fact that the feelings are out there gets kids in the habit of identifying and labeling their emotions. The kids say they like it. I do, too. It is also very portable.

These game meetings can be very productive problem solvers because they sometimes spark discussion of important issues. They also help by teaching everyone a lot more about incorporating feelings and emotional needs into everyday discussions. I guess that means the Family Forum is doing just what it was designed to do, building emotional bridges and proving that we consider each family member valuable enough to invest time in.

The Family Forum helps us get to know more about one another, how the others think and what they see as important. Tolerance grows with understanding. Clear values, priorities, and feelings set the stage for negotiation, compromise, and accountability with a minimum of resentment. The appreciation of each family member's basic right to love and respect is essential if the meeting is to be successful. In fact, there was a time when Todd couldn't do this.

"I sought professional help. Now that I am confident I can manage my anger, I recognize that the fact that conflicting needs exist does not grant license for me to verbally or emotionally abuse anyone. The family forum helps me to keep this in mind."

The meeting helps children and adolescents learn the pressures and responsibilities parents are held to as well. Understanding one another's pressures is a key to empathy. Empathy is not sympathy. Empathy is the capacity to experience what others feel, to put yourself in their place long enough to eliminate the distortions of mad self-talk. Rational, charitable reasoning allows you to objectively consider the merit of other viewpoints. Walking a mile or even a few seconds in little shoes changes one's perspective and aids problem solving.

Anger management is necessary for effective problem solving. Problem-solving skills will reduce the anger you feel that sometimes results from a sense of confusion or helplessness. You will learn how to transform the energy of anger into the energy of love. Active listening and speaking up in a timely fashion promote civility and trust. The Family Forum is a useful tool for those purposes. Anger will be less of a problem if there is mutual agreement on the rules for the Forum. By following the rules for fair fighting, the Family Forum can become a tool for problem solving instead of a free-for-all.

The C.O.O.L. Rules for the Family Forum follow guidelines I've found effective in my work with family meetings. If you can't decide who should speak first, roll the dice or pick a number. Each member rolls or picks. Highest number goes first. Each meeting can start off with a roll of the dice. The dice can help lighten things up and assure family members that they will have an equal opportunity to be heard first.

"I want my say." Okay, but let's set a timer and allow the members two minutes to make their points. When the time is up, next in line talks.

There should be free speech during Family Forum—no punishment for what is said or how it is said. This means kids, too. If kids don't like what they hear, they can't behave worse than normal after the family meeting. Of course, no spankings for what is said during meetings. The main guideline is protection. Be sure each family member promises that he or she will not punish or take revenge on another for what is said in the family meeting.

Praise first—you'll catch more bees with honey than you will with vinegar. So praise before you criticize. Positive before negative. Each member will be asked to describe something positive before he or she criticizes or raises a controversial issue for discussion. A positive approach will help to create an atmosphere of cooperation and trust. Trust will encourage open-minded consideration of others' opinions.

State an issue and stick to it—no topic changing. No museum tours or laundry lists of past problems or transgressions, as Dr. George Bach would say. He's the author of *The Intimate Enemy* and creator of a set of Rules for Fair Fighting that are very relevant today.

An issue can be anything that *any* family member feels strong about. An issue must pertain to relationships within the family. In other words, the issue to be discussed must involve the behavior, feelings, attitude, or values of a family member. As long as you are dealing with family members' feelings, ideas, attitudes, and values, you may discuss any topic that is relevant.

Be candid, truthful, but beware—words can wound. Words can also heal. Criticize ideas, not people. Criticize with compassion. "Yes, Camille, your brother really has feelings." Criticize with clarity, specific points, not generalizations. Criticize with charity. If it is impossible to criticize carefully, the help of a professional psychologist or therapist is indicated. Call one who is trained in family therapy.

Develop an agenda for family meetings. What type of meeting are you going to have—planning powwow, problem-solving session, or crisis council? The problem-focused meeting should have an agenda. Ask everyone for input. Write down the agenda of specific items that will be discussed. If the family situation is too explosive to have meaningful communication and problem solving, use the first meeting to set guidelines and an agenda for what will be discussed at the next meeting. An agenda is simply a list of issues much like the ones described earlier.

No long meetings. How long should the meetings be? Set a time limit. Plan at least twenty minutes and no longer than forty minutes for a Family Forum. Sunday night is a good time for many families, but anytime that is mutually convenient will do. Occasional, very occasional, longer meetings may be beneficial. Longer meetings should not be the rule. The length of the meetings will vary tremendously depending upon the age, patience, and activity level of the children and adults involved.

Remember, the Family Forum itself is one of the tools that is being used to help develop restraint. Family meetings also provide modeling and reinforcement of positive, constructive responses to stressful, difficult situations. In other words, the meeting has a main purpose of teaching problem-solving skills. The secondary purpose of the family meeting is to actually solve problems.

Bargain in good faith. When you strike a bargain, be sure you stick to it and hold other family members to their bargains. It is important that good faith be employed in family problem-solving sessions. Without good faith, the law of the jungle will prevail. Rule by power alone promotes chaos, not problem solving. Hopefully, regular meetings will promote social order. Confidence in the meeting system will be lost without evidence of good faith in family problem solving. Using the Family Forum to manipulate the family trust by admitting misdeeds and claiming sanctuary would be considered operating in bad faith.

Watch your words. Rotary International, a huge charitable organization, one of the largest in the world, has developed the Four Way Test. The Four Way Test is designed to encourage constructive communication. Your family might want to apply the Four Way Test to what is said at family meetings.

The Four Way Test is really a series of questions to promote reflective thinking. It is spoken aloud at the beginning of each Rotary meeting to help members be mindful of the power of their words.

- Is it the truth?
- Is it fair to all concerned?
- Will it build goodwill?
- Will it be beneficial to all concerned?

The Rotary Four Way Test is designed to promote positive, healthy communication among members. Rotary is an organization of business and professional leaders, men and women with strong egos, all of whom are used to being in positions of power and being listened to. In the family setting, we, too, have strong egos. We all want to be recognized and we all believe what we have to say is of utmost importance. We all believe we are right! If we use the Four Way Test to remind us that other family members feel similarly about the importance of their ideas, perhaps problem solving and conflict resolution will become easier.

Afterword

Most of us who are raising challenging children get very down on ourselves. I've seen it over and over again in my work as a psychologist, and as a parent I've felt it.

Parents, your children's behavior, public and private, has a great deal of influence on how you feel about yourself. The product of your own bodies, hearts, and minds will always influence your feelings about yourself. It would be unrealistic to think you could detach your self-esteem totally from that of your children. It would be unnatural to do so, if you could. As you learn ways to nourish your self-esteem, you will feel more adequate as a person regardless of the successes or failures of your children.

High-energy kids underscore the need to get away, to get a break. Identify competent care givers and use them! Take time off for an afternoon, weekend, or week, but please take it. Plan for respite care as part of your budget. It is important to make time for yourself. It is also important to make time to develop your relationship with your spouse.

Difficult children strain the spousal relationship, even destroy it, because you get so drained. You become stressed out, worrying so much about the children that you no longer have energy for each other. You argue with each other about how to take care of the children. Your love and compassion for the children will erode and may eventually even destroy the love you once felt for each other. A family violence survey I reviewed recently indicated that parents assault each other most often because of disagreements about children's behavior. Whatever you do, as you continue along your journey to become a better and more effective parent, be sure to take time to nourish yourself emotionally. Take care of yourself, and take care of the important relationships in your life. You are worth it.

Appendix

If you suspect, or have been told, that your child might have any sort of attention-deficit disorder, here are the guidelines that will be used to evaluate them.

DSM-IV DIAGNOSIS—DEFINITIONS

Diagnostic criteria for Attention-Deficit/Hyperactivity Disorder

A. Either (1) or (2):
 (1) six (or more) of the following symptoms of inattention have persisted for at least 6 months to a degree that is maladaptive and inconsistent with developmental level:
 Inattention
 (a) often fails to give close attention to details or makes careless mistakes in schoolwork, work, or other activities
 (b) often has difficulty sustaining attention in tasks or play activities
 (c) often does not seem to listen when spoken to directly
 (d) often does not follow through on instructions and fails to finish schoolwork, chores, or duties in the workplace (not due to oppositional behavior or failure to understand instructions)
 (e) often has difficulty organizing tasks and activities
 (f) often avoids, dislikes, or is reluctant to engage in tasks that require sustained mental effort (such as schoolwork or homework)
 (g) often loses things necessary for tasks or activities (e.g., toys, school assignments, pencils, books, or tools)
 (h) is often easily distracted by extraneous stimuli

   (i) is often forgetful in daily activities
  (2) six (or more) of the following symptoms of hyperactivity-impulsivity have persisted for at least 6 months to a degree that is maladaptive and inconsistent with developmental level:
   Hyperactivity
   (a) often fidgets with hands or feet or squirms in seat
   (b) often leaves seat in classroom or in other situations in which remaining seated is expected
   (c) often runs about or climbs excessively in situations in which it is inappropriate (in adolescents or adults, may be limited to subjective feelings of restlessness)
   (d) often has difficulty playing or engaging in leisure activities quietly
   (e) is often "on the go" or often acts as if "driven by a motor"
   (f) often talks excessively
   Impulsivity
   (g) often blurts out answers before questions have been completed
   (h) often has difficulty awaiting turn
   (i) often interrupts or intrudes on others (e.g., butts into conversations or games)

B. Some hyperactive-impulsive or inattentive symptoms that caused impairment were present before age 7 years.

C. Some impairment from the symptoms is present in two or more settings (e.g., at school, work, and at home).

D. There must be clear evidence of clinically significant impairment in social, academic, or occupational functioning.

Diagnostic criteria for Conduct Disorder

A. A repetitive and persistent pattern of behavior in which the basic rights of others or major age-appropriate societal norms or rules are violated, as manifested by the presence of three (or more) of the following criteria in the past 12 months, with at least one criterion present in the past 6 months:
 Aggression to people and animals
 (1) often bullies, threatens, or intimidates others
 (2) often initiates physical fights

(3) has used a weapon that can cause serious physical harm to others (e.g., a bat, brick, broken bottle, knife, gun)

(4) has been physically cruel to people

(5) has been physically cruel to animals

(6) has stolen while confronting a victim (e.g., mugging, purse snatching, extortion, armed robbery)

(7) has forced someone into sexual activity

Destruction of property

(8) has deliberately engaged in fire setting with the intention of causing serious damage

(9) has deliberately destroyed others' property (other than by fire setting)

Deceitfulness or theft

(10) has broken into someone else's house, building, or car

(11) often lies to obtain goods or favors or to avoid obligations (i.e., "cons" others)

(12) has stolen items of nontrivial value without confronting a victim (e.g., shoplifting, but without breaking and entering; forgery)

Serious violations of rules

(13) often stays out at night despite parental prohibitions, beginning before age 13 years

(14) has run away from home overnight at least twice while living in parental or parental surrogate home (or once without returning for a lengthy period)

(15) is often truant from school, beginning before age 13 years

B. The disturbance in behavior causes clinically significant impairment in social, academic, or occupational functioning.

C. If the individual is age 18 years or older, criteria are not met for Antisocial Personality Disorder.

Diagnostic criteria for Oppositional Defiant Disorder

A. A pattern of negativistic, hostile, and defiant behavior lasting at least 6 months, during which four (or more) of the following are present:

(1) often loses temper

(2) often argues with adults

    (3) often actively defies or refuses to comply with adults' re-
        quests or rules
    (4) often deliberately annoys people
    (5) often blames others for his or her mistakes or misbehavior
    (6) is often touchy or easily annoyed by others
    (7) is often angry and resentful
    (8) is often spiteful or vindictive

Note: Consider a criterion met only if the behavior occurs more frequently than is typically observed in individuals of comparable age
and developmental level.

B. The disturbance in behavior causes clinically significant impair-
    ment in social, academic, or occupational functioning.

C. The behaviors do not occur exclusively during the course of a
    Psychotic or Mood Disorder.

D. Criteria are not met for Conduct Disorder, and, if the individual
    is age 18 years or older, criteria are not met for Antisocial Per-
    sonality Disorder.

E. The symptoms do not occur exclusively during the course of a
    Pervasive Developmental Disorder, Schizophrenia, or other Psy-
    chotic Disorder and are not better accounted for by another
    mental disorder (e.g., Mood Disorder, Anxiety Disorder, Disso-
    ciative Disorder, or a Personality Disorder).

Services Available

Dr. Makarowski offers state-of-the-art consulting services, most notably workshops and seminars in the areas of parenting, sports and peak performance, as well as stress and anger management. Programs are custom tailored to your organization's specific needs.

Self-instructional audio cassette programs are also available, as well as other skill-oriented materials that serve as a follow-up support system.

Dr. Makarowski is also the author of "Tips for Success in Sports and Life," an exciting and dynamic column that gives you specific concrete skills for utilizing psychology on an everyday, practical basis.

If you would like to arrange for Dr. Makarowski to speak to your organization, or are interested in other materials, you can contact him through:

Perigee Books   or   Louis M. Makarowski,
The Berkley Publishing Group   Ph.D., & Associates
200 Madison Avenue   5120 Bayou Boulevard
New York, N.Y. 10016   Suite 6
                                           Pensacola, FL 32503

Positive Parenting

__20 Teachable Virtues: Practical Ways to Pass on
Lessons of Virtue and Character to Your Children**
by Barbara C. Unell and Jerry L. Wyckoff, Ph.D. 0-399-51959-9/$10.00
A plan for parents to encourage moral excellence in their children and
incorporate virtue into day-to-day family life.

__The Art of Sensitive Parenting: The 10 Keys to
Raising Confident, Competent, and Responsible Children**
by Katharine C. Kersey, Ed.D. 0-425-14432-1/$10.95
A breakthrough program for fostering confidence and independence
from expert Katharine Kersey.

__The Challenging Child**
by Mitch Golant, Ph.D. and Donna Corwin 0-425-14953-6/$10.95
Wise, practical advice about dealing with nonconforming children in
ways that maintain discipline and encourage maturity.

__Don't Take It Out on Your Kids!**
by Katharine C. Kersey, Ed.D. 0-425-14372-4/$10.00
A new approach to discipline including creating a bond of trust,
keeping anger in check, and more.

__Families Apart: 10 Keys to Successful Co-Parenting**
by Melinda Blau 0-399-52150-X/$12.00
Ten solid principles to enable divorced parents and their children to
function as a family even though they no longer live together.

__Helping Your Child Handle Stress**
by Katharine C. Kersey, Ed.D. 0-425-14540-9/$10.00
This guide explains how parents can provide comfort and support
when their children are faced with the issues that affect them strongly.

__Teaching Peace: How to Raise Children in Harmony
Without Prejudice, Fear, or Violence**
by Jan Arnow 0-399-52155-0/$12.00
An essential action guide for parents, teachers and community leaders
on raising children to eliminate prejudice, embrace differences, and
end violence.